50p

(1)

New

Tried By Fire

N Ireland

Tried by Fire

Finding Hope Out of Suffering In Northern Ireland

ALF McCREARY

Marshall Pickering

Marshall Morgan and Scott
Marshall Pickering
3 Beggarwood Lane, Basingstoke,
Hants RG23 7LP, UK

British Library Cataloguing in Publication Data

Tried by fire: finding hope out of
    suffering in Northern Ireland.—
    2nd ed.
    1. Northern Ireland—Social conditions
    —1969–
    I. McCreary Alf. Profiles of hope
    941.60824   HN398.N6

    ISBN 0–551–01343–5

Text set in Century Roman (face) by Input Typeset-
ting Ltd, London
Printed in Great Britain by Hazell Watson & Viney
Ltd, Member of the BPCC Group, Aylesbury, Bucks.

Dedicated to Nannie Doctor
who knew about Peacemaking

Contents

Acknowledgements

Grateful acknowledgement is made for the quotation from the New English Bible and to the Executor of W. B. Yeats for the quotation from The Lake Isle of Innisfree.

The author would like to thank the many people involved in the origin and preparation of this book. They include those who took the time and in some cases the trouble to talk about their experiences; Maureen Dickson, Ann-Marie Reade and Debbie McAleese, who helped with the transcripts and typing; and Hilary McCreary who once again took a deep breath and lived with all the circumstances and pressures that surround an idea until it eventually becomes a book.

Foreword
by
The Most Reverend Robert Runcie, Archbishop of Canterbury

The suffering of the people in Ireland, both in the North and South, has continued for so long that there may be some who would be tempted to think the situation was hopeless. Constantly the headlines tell the story of violence and tragedy. Those who know Ireland know well that this is only a part of the picture. Men, women and young people across the country refuse to give way to despair, and Alf McCreary has done us all a service by recording these stories of hope, courage and faith in the future.

I warmly commend this book to your careful reading and also ask you to continue with me in praying for a peaceful and just resolution to problems which can be solved, providing we maintain faith, hope and a continuing love for our fellow men and women.

Robert Cantuar
Lambeth Palace
August, 1985

Preface

Some time ago, my elder son Mark came home from school in Belfast and informed me that my book *Profiles of Hope* was still being used in the classroom by one of the religious education teachers. A week or so later, a contributor to the BBC Radio Four programme 'Thought for the Day' asked my permission to quote a short section from the book.

These two references to the book, both within a short period, confirmed my experience that people were still talking about *Profiles of Hope*, which was published several years ago and which was virtually out of print. I felt that a re-issue of the book would meet a need, which was becoming more apparent as the existing supply of books trickled to a mere handful. With the valued assistance of Mr John Hunt, Managing Director of Marshall Pickering Holdings Ltd, and Mr William Fitch, a mutual friend, this new edition has become a reality.

The current volume is a reprint of *Profiles of Hope*, with some new and important material. This includes contributions from the Countess Mountbatten of Burma, Mr Terry Waite, and two former Ulster paramilitaries who were converted to Christianity while in prison. The new section also includes a foreword from the Archbishop of Canterbury, who quoted extensively from *Profiles of Hope* during a televised sermon from Belfast Cathedral. He visited Northern Ireland shortly after he took up office.

The original material published in *Profiles of Hope* remains unchanged, apart from some minimal up-dating. The copy is otherwise timeless, because I believe that the sentiments expressed by those involved will live on to inspire others in similar circumstances.

In one sense, this is not my book. It is the work of those whose individual and collective experience has something significant to contribute to the search for peace. I am extremely grateful that this publication will allow their words, and the words of others, to live on.

Alf McCreary
1 January 1986

Introduction: People Matter Most

Terry Waite is the Archbishop of Canterbury's Advisor on Anglican Communion Affairs. In this role he has been involved in a number of delicate initiatives, requiring great diplomacy, to release hostages in areas of potential or actual civil conflict. During the Christmas and New Year period of 1980 Mr Waite was in Iran, at the height of the Ayatollah Khomeini revolution, to talk to Government officials about the release of four Britons and four Iranian church members. They included three missionaries and a businessman. All four had been held without charges, for several months. After protracted discussions with the Iranian Government, the three missionaries were released. The businessman and the Iranians were also released.

In 1984, again during the Christmas and New Year period, Mr Waite went to Libya to talk to Colonel Gadaffi and the Libyan authorities about the release of four Britons, who had been detained without charges for nearly five months. The talks took place at a particularly sensitive time. Britain had severed diplomatic relations with Libya, following the murder of Woman Police Constable Yvonne Fletcher who was shot by an unknown gunman from the sanctuary of the Libyan Embassy in London, earlier in 1984. WPC Fletcher and her colleagues had been policing a demonstration at the Embassy in April, when a marksman from inside the building gunned her down without warning. Mr Waite's discussions with the

Libyans several months later were protracted and
difficult, and frequently they took place within the
glare of television cameras. Eventually the four
Britons were released.

In 1985, Mr. Waite risked personal danger when he
visited war-ravaged Lebanon to negotiate on behalf of
American hostages held there.

Terry Waite is a tall, striking figure. He has worked
as an advisor to the Bishop of Bristol. He spent three
years in Uganda, during the regime of Idi Amin, and
then seven years in Rome, co-ordinating educational
and development programmes for the Roman Catholic
Church. In March 1980 he joined the Archbishop of
Canterbury's staff as international affairs advisor.

Terry Waite has considerable experience of conflict
situations, and he has a deep interest in Irish affairs.
His wife, Frances, is a Belfast girl. They were married
in 1964, and Terry Waite has been in Ulster many
times. In this chapter he reflects, in a personal interview, on the problems of Ireland, North and South,
not only from his international experience, but also
from a local perspective.

I AM not a stranger to Ulster. I have known it for
almost a quarter of a century. I have had close
contact and I have been there very regularly over
those years. Of course, I knew Belfast before the
onset of these recent troubles. One of the things that
one needs to recognise is that every excellent and
positive attribute in people – be they British,
English, Irish, Scottish or Welsh or any other nation
– has its opposite side. On the positive side the
people of Northern Ireland are quite exceptional and
remarkable for their straightforward loyalty and for
their openness and friendliness and for their decent
and good qualities. Those are shorthand ways of
expressing a great deal. Of course they do have,

and probably have had to develop over the years, a
unique determination in order to survive. In a sense
the opposite side of loyalty could sometimes be
beyond determination. It could be almost a stubbornness. Stubbornness itself is not necessarily a
bad thing, but it can be a factor in human relationships which makes for certain difficulties in
communication. I do not write it off entirely as a
negative quality. Nobody from outside Northern
Ireland should be arrogant enough to think that
they have a solution to the problems of Northern
Ireland, nor should they in any way pontificate. All
they can do is make simple observations based on
experience, and relate other experiences which they
have had to that particular situation.

It seems to me that the only way in which the
problem facing the people of Ireland is to be resolved
is by individuals recognising that they have the
power to change and transform a situation which
appears impossible. The situation is not impossible.
No human situation that has been created by men
is impossible to redeem. If that were the case, then
we all might as well give up. The temptation is to
think that it is only those who have positions of
authority or power who can bring about change.
That is not true. Those who have positions of authority and power have been given, or have taken,
positions of special responsibility, but the real key
to change lies in the hands of every man and woman
who is living in that situation.

It seems to me also that the way, or one way, to
approach the problem is to have a profound respect
for the other person. The Protestant must have a
profound respect for the Catholic and vice versa. On
what is that respect based? You base it on a very
simple platform of human dignity, that the other

person has as much right to walk this earth as I
have, and on a very basic religious premise that the
other person is just as much a child of God as I am.
They may think differently, they may act differently, they may behave differently and they may
have different values, all those things may be
different, but they are human beings wth a right to
live. Having said that and having recognised that
there are differences, then we are faced with the
problem of having to live with difference. Secondly,
how do we turn it into creative difference rather
than allowing it to be destructive and negative? It
is far too easy to allow difference to become negative
and destructive, rather than to seek it out and
enable it to become fulfilling and positive. In no
way must one simply point to Ireland. There are
examples one can draw from New Zealand and
Australia with the aboriginal communities, Canada
which has groups with different aspirations, and
particularly the Middle East where people of
different religious, ethnic and social backgrounds,
are struggling with this problem.

I also see this to a certain degree in England, so
the question comes nearer home – how do you
enable difference to be creative? Based on those
premises of profound respect for each other, and the
recognition of difference, one has to see points of
commonality. Let me take another example of
working for improved understanding between Islam
and Christianity. There are a great number of
points where we would disagree, but let us for a
moment concentrate on the point where we do agree.
In some negotiations I have stressed that both Christians and Muslims believe in a God who is a God
of mercy, of compassion and of justice. These are
basic points of agreement.

This applied particularly during my negotiations in Libya for the release of the British hostages. First of all Colonel Gadaffi had to be reasonably convinced that in so far as I gave him my word, I would do my utmost to keep it. I had to be able to have enough trust to say that in so far as he gave me his word, he would also keep it. We sought to establish some common ground. I promised nothing that I couldn't deliver and I told him quite clearly that the church could not interfere with, nor have power over, the law of the United Kingdom, that those facing prosecution in this country would have to be subject to the process of our law. However, I did say that we could do our best to see that Libyan people in Britain were treated humanely and fairly, and we are still trying to do that. So one had to have a basis of trust. What so often happens in the world today is that we get into polarized situations and begin to drift apart so that there is no, or there seems to be no possibility of creating a bond whereby people can learn to trust. This is one reason why, for example, I am pleased to support the Corrymeela Community in Northern Ireland which does attempt, in its own way, to bring people together from different sections of society. Those who have been bereaved or those who have been touched by violence in one way or another, are brought together to enable them to share common experiences, sometimes common experiences which are very bitter and to recognize always that in the middle of political, economic, religious, and ethnic differences, it really is human beings that count, human beings that matter, feelings that matter, people being hurt that matter. Those are the things that matter.

That is the way I approached Colonel Gadaffi, as a person, and I refused to be trapped by stereotypes.

That means taking a risk. The danger of stereotypes
is that if you trap people and do not allow them to
move, there is no possibility of dialogue. You have
to be prepared to let me move from where you
thought I was, to another position. The same is true
of myself, I have to let the other person move from
a position in which they have been stereotyped, into
another position, to give room for movement in
dialogue. There is no substitute for that.

I had to learn that Colonel Gadaffi, coming from
his culture, had a different attitude towards decision
making and a different approach to a number of
questions. He had a different attitude to decision
making, though it doesn't mean to say that it was
better or worse than my attitude. I had to understand his attitude towards decision-making, and he
had to try and understand mine. We were then in
a better position to make a decision together. You
have to check assumptions and you have to take
time in the dialogue to understand another point of
view. Some people find that difficult, or else they
are too threatened to understand another position,
or they have suffered too much, or they have been
let down. It is a very bitter and painful experience
if you have given your hand in trust to somebody
and suddenly they turn round and they stab you.
That is very painful. To give trust, to have understanding, is quite costly.

We faced considerable difficulties in Libya. Diplomatic relations had been broken with this country.
People in Britain were extremely upset and angry
at the shooting of WPC Fletcher. Libyans in this
country were on trial for terrorist charges, accused
of engaging in terrorism. All those factors meant
that the situation was highly explosive and very
volatile and not an easy one in which to walk. A

false move could have led to very serious repercussions, either personal or political, or repercussions that would affect a lot of people. So it was
dangerous and difficult. It was a strain, not an
unmanageable strain, but a recognition of a
responsibility and a recognition that one had to be,
in that situation, out on a limb, one had to be fairly
self sufficient and self-reliant. I had to be able to
take decisions and stand by those decisions for what
they were.

I sometimes thought that it might not work out
but it was very important for me to say that, regardless of the situation, I would ask the Libyan people
to do their best to follow the three principles that I
had agreed with Colonel Gadaffi. These were the
principles of compassion, justice, and of mercy. So I
continually hoped that they would do their best; I
think they did.

I think on the whole that the British hostages
managed very well, but I think there were times
when they were fairly low in spirit and wondered if
they would ever be freed from that situation. There
are very, very dark periods for everyone in life and
periods of great strain, trial and stress. If one didn't
have hope then it would be a very bleak picture
indeed. Hope is central to the Christian faith. It is
something which constantly has to be held on to,
even when you have difficulty in feeling it. Whilst
feelings are important, they are not the only guide.
Sometimes we need to know that central to our faith
lies hope. It is there for us to grasp hold of even
though the outcome is not always what we had
expected. Hope remains eternal.

I am referring to simple human hope which takes
into account forms of experience which include all
human aspirations. If we have to analyse that more

clearly, we have to ask ourselves certain questions. What is it we are aspiring to? Do we really want peace? Do we really want wholeness? If we want wholeness for ourselves and for our immediate family, the first recognition is that wholeness can never be taken as something that is exclusive. My wholeness is dependent upon my relationship with my neighbour.

Wholeness, and fulfilment is related to wholeness and fulfilment of community. That is just another way of saying that no man is an island. He is intimately related to others. His wholeness depends on that. That is why it is so important, particularly in this day and age that we give attention to the building and creating of a healthy community so that we can be related in a healthy and whole way to it. If you really say you want personal wholeness, you are bound to be concerned about the welfare of the total community, even the welfare of those in that total community whom you disagree with and sometimes disapprove of. That takes us back to the argument about creative difference.

In Libya what I wanted more than anything else was agreement with honour. I wanted an agreement that honoured the Libyan people and an agreement that honoured our own people. I think that this was achieved. I would not have been happy about going into Libya and trying to make other people with different views to my own look small or silly, because they are not small or silly people. There are a lot of very remarkable and very fine people in Libya. I do not deny that there have been difficulties. I do not deny that there have been acts of terrorism. I disagree, strongly disagree with the use of violence as a means of settling disputes and differences between people, because I think violence breeds violence. Having said all that, I am not prepared to belittle other people. One tries to understand and to recognise fundamentally that at the end of the day the power of love is greater than the power of the gun. If people have a truly religious outlook they will hold on to that and recognise that.

I don't think that the British hostages in Libya were religious people as such, but they all had some touch with religion at some time or point in their lives. When they were isolated together in Libya, several of them said how they had prayed. It was actually the first time in many, many years that they were conscious of a presence with them which they hadn't been conscious of before. I think also it meant a lot to them when we had our Christmas service conducted under fairly difficult and extreme circumstances.

Several years earlier I faced another extremely difficult situation with British hostages in Iran. Working there with revolutionary guards I wanted to understand what it was that was motivating them and where we had points of agreement before going further. A lot of people in this world are smarting under what they see to be a deep, deep sense of injustice, a deep sense of being constantly and totally wronged by big powers, a deep feeling of always being pushed about by people who have power and authority in this world, or governments with power and authority, and then they often react in an aggressive and violent manner. We have to examine this and ask what truth is there in this. Are people being pushed around, are they being treated as less than human? If you find the answer to that is 'yes' then you are obliged to say that this is wrong. We have got to examine what it is that causes people, often very decent people, to be pushed to a point, an extreme position. What is it that causes people to engage in violence and acts of terrorism in an almost calculated, unthinking, unfeeling way? How is it that people get into the grip of that sort of thing? Often when you ask such questions, the reasons you discover may be unpalatable. Are the reasons valid, do they hold up? If they are, what can be done to change them so that people can be accorded their total and proper human dignity? Those are often complicated and difficult questions to ask and to answer.

I work intuitively, but intuition has to be matched with reason and common sense. Very often in this type of situation where normal mechanisms and structures of government or diplomacy become locked or blocked, a person with intuition can cut across barriers or channels that might have become blocked or hardened, and cut straight through.

The basic problem in Iran was that the church was accused of engaging in operations against the state. In other words, the Christians were accused of spying. These accusations later on proved to be totally false. Part of my job was to help them to be proved false, because I knew they were nonsense from the start. Once we got to that point, then people were released. It took an awful lot of doing but, in that revolutionary situation anyone who has any association, however tenuous, with people outside the country, often falls under suspicion.

The situation in Iran was dangerous.

There is always danger when people are walking around with loaded automatics. I was being taken to interrogation camps and around the city at a time of great excitement, but again I was willing to enter into a relationship with revolutionary guards. Therefore I had to be prepared to trust them. If I

wasn't prepared to trust them then I felt that I ought
not to be there. I just had to put my life in their
hands. They honoured that.

I have worked in a lot of these difficult situations,
as well as in Iran and Libya which have brought me
personal and public prominence. There have been a
lot of other situations. Some have been successful
and some have not. Nobody can achieve 'success'
every time. I cannot and I don't think many other
people can. I don't have an inflated opinion of my
own ability in these matters. I just do what I can.

There are times when you have to go public, but
I think often in many situations it is just as
important, if not more important, to work quietly
behind the scenes. It depends on the situation. It is
always important to seek guidance through prayer.

If prayer means anything, it means a way of life,
not just an activity within life. It implies an orientation of life towards certain ends, and that in itself
is constantly sustaining. I am often asked, 'Do you
tend to pray more if you are in a crisis situation?' I
don't think I do. Perhaps my mind might be more
concentrated, but I think prayer has to be something
that is constant, that gives an orientation and then
becomes a way of life. It is certainly a sustaining
factor.

One is also sustained by the immediate family
and by one or two close friends. I think this friendship is a precious – and a costly – thing. If you are
going to have friendship, then you have got to be
prepared to give and to receive. At times of difficulty
it can be very sustaining and creative, even if you
are out of touch with your friends and your family.
It is also important to recognise that one is
sustained and supported by the Archbishop and his
staff. I am very much a member of a team. I am not

just an individual, and that is important. Then, in
those public events like Libya and Iran I was always
conscious of being very much supported by the
people of the United Kingdom, who I think in the
main wanted to see a decent and fair outcome to the
matter. I was very conscious of that sort of support.
I was also conscious of the support of many people
in Libya. A lot of people said, 'We want this to
be cleared up'. Libyan people came up to me and
congratulated me, and said, 'Well done, we are very
pleased'. That in itself was sustaining.

However, there is a deeper dimension to all of
this. Someone once said to me, 'Have you stopped to
consider why it is that you are often dealing with
conflict situations?' When I thought about it, I recognised that one reason why I had been concerned
about reconciliation and healing in the world, was
because I have been seeking the reconciliation and
healing within myself. When I look into myself I
recognise that I am a peculiar and complicated
mixture of what is light and what is dark. What
could happen is that the light and the dark become
so separated from one another that you are torn
apart. I think within one's inner personal life, one
has to be constantly, gradually and gently working
for that inner harmony, that inner healing, which
isn't achieved in a week or a year. It is something
that is the work of a lifetime. There is no way in
which you can work for the reconciliation and
healing of others unless you are working on your
own inner healing and reconciliation. It is a very,
very difficult process. I think that you cannot take
a step out into the world, for that is the correct
terminology to use, unless you are prepared to take
an equal step within yourself. The area where the
greatest reconciliation needs to take place is within

those deep and hidden areas of the soul where the
great battles are fought, where inspiration and
depression co-exist, where all the seed bed of action
is rooted, in the recesses of the soul. At the end of
the day that is the most important area.

In recognising and dealing with situations, one is
recognising constantly that here is a man with a
son or here is a mother who has just had her son
murdered, or here is a brother whose sister has been
treated desperately. People, people, people ... all
the time suffering in the inner agonies of their soul.
The spiritual questions are the fundamental questions of this world. This is not easily recognised in
a secular world. It is very difficult to touch in a
world where everyone has forgotten the language of
spiritual insight and understanding, or have never
learned it. But even if you have never learned a
language, this is all the more reason for us to have
interpreters and all the more reason for clergy to be
truly physicians of the soul, and not be seduced into
the role of becoming politicians.

All of this, I believe, is of relevance to Ireland.

All the qualities that go to make a fine, a wholesome and a healthy community lie there. They are
often given expression, and often they lie clouded.
The key lies with the people of Ireland themselves.
It is the people of Ireland who will have to resolve
these problems, and they will do so.

Those people who have known the greatest
suffering are the ones who have the potential and
understanding of the greatness of love and the
healing power of love. It is the complacent and the
arrogant and the seemingly self-sufficient who are
probably a long way from the Kingdom. Those who
have known something of bitterness are also those
who also can know its opposite in terms of knowing

something of love and creativity, and the real
meaning of redemption. A problem for people who
intuitively know religion, which would be applicable
to all of us, is that they can sometimes just get a
little trapped in the formula and language and
perhaps fail to recognise these are simply the structure, and that the essence lies in the depth of
meaning and the practical application of love and
understanding and mutual recognition and respect.
It is at that level where you face the hard demands
of the Gospel. The hard demands are not to get up
and go to church every Sunday. The hard demands
come in the words of our Lord, 'Love your neighbour
as yourself'. That is probably the hardest demand
facing every person who walks the soil of Ireland,
who claims to love the soil of Ireland. It is not just
love your territory, it is love your neighbour.

2

Behind the Headlines

Alf McCreary is an award-winning writer who covered the Ulster story from Belfast since the outbreak of the troubles in 1968. He has written in detail about the violence, the attempts at a political settlement, and the work of the peace-makers in both main communities.

He has also travelled widely in Europe, Africa, Asia and Latin-America, and his work in the Third World (about which he has written the book, *Up-With People*) has given him an opportunity to view Irish affairs from a global perspective.

He spent more than two decades with the *Belfast Telegraph* as a specialist writer, columnist and commentator. He has also written extensively for a range of newspapers and publications in the British Isles, Europe and the United States. He received a number of awards and commendations for his work as a journalist. These included two British National Press Awards and several Northern Ireland Press Awards, including the title 'Rothman's Journalist of the Year'. Mr McCreary lives in Belfast with his wife Hilary, and their children Emma-Jane, Mark and Matthew.

THE PROCESS of inquiring about Ireland, North and South, has been likened to peeling an onion. As one layer is removed, another layer comes into view. Taken to a logical conclusion this could mean

that at the heart of this Irish onion there is nothing
at all, other than a mess of discarded layers. Yet
there is a core and a reality at the heart of Irish
affairs but any attempt to penetrate to this reality
will include an element of messiness and not a few
tears. Peeling an onion, like writing about political
events and violence in Ireland, is not always the
most sociable and pleasant of tasks.

This, however, does not seem to daunt many
observers inside and outside Ireland who have
written exhaustively about the religious, cultural,
economic and political dimensions to the conflict.
Indeed if analyses of Irish affairs were the keys to
prosperity and peace, there would be no shortage of
solutions. Despite the inventiveness of man, and the
inventiveness of so many Irish men and women in
so many other fields, this bitter quarrel lingers on
towards the 21st century with a peculiar integrity
that few other races can match. The Irish are said
to be a caring people. Perhaps they care too much
when some are prepared to kill others to make a
political point.

Part of the tragedy is that the conflict feeds on
itself. Today's generation of young people has grown
up in a political wilderness that is pockmarked by
bomb and bullet. Many children are the prisoners
of their own environment and are programmed by
their background to support one side or the other.
There are, of course, children and parents who take
the positive view and who try to escape from the
shackles of the past to bring some objectivity to the
present. But the peace-makers in Ireland, North and
South, face a formidable task in trying to nurture
the tender plant of reason and understanding in a
cold and often hostile climate.

Another contributory factor in the Irish conflict is

that each person, like each group, sees that conflict in his or her own terms. The Northern Protestant argues that he has the democratic majority in Northern Ireland and that he therefore has the right to majority rule. And he would regard the aspirations of Northern Roman Catholics for a United Ireland as nothing less than treachery and a lack of loyalty to the Northern state.

The Southern Republican would argue that the Northern Protestant is less than reasonable in refusing to share the top positions of power and influence with Northern Catholics in a Belfast-based government which would have certain powers transferred from Westminster. Furthermore he would point out that this system of devolved or transferred government had not worked properly and that the real root of the Irish conflict is the Northern Protestant's stubbornness in refusing to take part in an all-Ireland government. Why should one million Northerners, who are a minority on the island, hold out against the wishes of a majority of people in Ireland?

In reply the Northerner would say that he does not trust the Southerner and that he is afraid of entering into partnership in a State which is so heavily disposed to the power of the Roman Catholic Church. Whether these fears are justified or not is scarcely the point, disappointing though that might seem. In Ireland, North and South, and for all kinds of Irishmen and women it is important to know the relevance of Murphy's Law of Communication; 'What people believe to be the truth is more potent and often more dangerous than the truth itself.'

So the old arguments continue, often with only a nodding acquaintance with the true facts of history and contemporary events. But the impact of this

partial view of Irish affairs cannot be over-
estimated.

(This was demonstrated forcibly on a study-tour
to Holland by six journalists from Northern Ireland
and six from the Republic. Three each were asked
to take over the roles of management, Press, trade
unions and international directors in an imaginary
take-over of a local firm by a multinational. After
an evening of intensive role-playing, the authen-
ticity of which surprised even those hard-bitten
professionals, the message was made clear by the
Dutch hosts – each group in the game was seeing
the conflict only in its own terms. No-one had been
able to stand back and take the global view. The
parallel with the Irish conflict was all too real.)

In Ireland the conflict is so complex that people
will disagree about the relative importance of the
contributory factors. Some will point to religion,
others to cultural differences, others to economics,
and others still to political conflicts. Some will list
more than one cause, but in different degrees of
importance. Any simple analysis is mistrusted
mainly because it seems too simple. The Irish are a
rhetorical race who look for complexities that will
measure up to their eloquence. As the British and
others have found out, if something appears simple
the Irish will soon make it complicated.

Religion is a factor in the conflict, though some
churchmen would claim that this is over-stressed.
Certainly there is broad agreement that the fight is
not about theology as such. The days are gone when
people are burned at the stake for a refusal to accept
a tenet of what is thought to be the true faith. It is
beyond dispute that stone-throwing mobs in Belfast
and Londonderry are not pelting one another or the

police to make a point about the Virgin Birth or transubstantiation.

It would be misleading to suggest, however, that religion is not therefore a factor to be taken seriously. There are many Protestants who would be fearful, rightly or wrongly, of the influence of the Roman Catholic Church and who see the Irish conflict in terms of a Vatican conquest that has to be resisted at all costs. There is, equally, a Roman Catholic mistrust and fear of a Protestant majority in a Northern state that would favour Presbyterians, Anglicans and Methodists at the expense of Roman Catholics. And in an all-Ireland context, Northern Protestants could look with distrust on a theocracy where divorce is prohibited and contraception is limited.

Thus if religion in the conflict is not strictly theological, it is certainly tribal. In Northern Ireland the terms 'Roman Catholic' and 'Protestant' immediately suggest different backgrounds, cultures and values. The Catholic is likely to have been given a thorough grounding in history as seen from a Catholic Irish point of view, and to speak, to whatever degree, the Irish language. He or she is likely to play or have played essentially Irish games like Gaelic football, hurling, and camogie.

The Protestant, by contrast, is likely to have a grounding in history as seen from a British point of view and is unlikely to be able to speak even a smattering of the Irish language, or to play Gaelic games. Of course there are exceptions. Some Protestants speak Gaelic, some Catholics will have gone to a Protestant school and will have read history through Protestant eyes. Protestants and Catholics share a number of sports and activities, particularly in middle-class areas and professions. But in the

main the cultural divide between Protestants and
Catholics remains.

It is immensely sad that such a degree of mutual
ignorance still exists. One of the major problems of
Northern Ireland and of Ireland as a whole is that
so few people know how the others live. This is
particularly clear to me as I cross the barriers in
the North, and often the Irish border into the South.
It is fair to say that many in the Republic who talk
about Irish unity have not been to the North and
know little or nothing about the Northern Protestant. In the same vein, the Unionists in the North
who cling to loyalty to Britain are not knowledge-
able about the South, though more seem to travel
to the Republic than Southerners come North.

In the North itself the mutual ignorance of both
communities about one another is depressing. This
may not be apparent to those who pontificate from
the familiarity of their own backgrounds and who
remain fortified by their own herd instinct. But to
me, this mutual lack of knowledge is very apparent.
A reporter can sit in the Catholic Bogside of Derry
and take tea with an unemployed Derry man who
will talk with passion and conviction about the
rights and wrongs of history and the brighter future
in a United Ireland. The same reporter the next day
can sit in Protestant East Belfast and take tea with
an unemployed ship-builder who will talk with
equal conviction and passion about the rights and
wrongs of history and about the advantages of main-
taining the link with Britain.

One particular meeting with a Catholic Derryman
and a Protestant from Belfast was, for me, a salutary lesson. During dinner they talked about work
and the lack of work in Northern Ireland. They
found that, as working men, they had much in

common but once they switched to politics the
barriers went up and there was no more communication. They were talking at one another and not to
one another, and sadly they symbolised the division
between their communities which, on a purely economic basis in a deprived part of the United
Kingdom, have so much in common, namely unemployment and lower living standards than in the
rest of the United Kingdom.

Some observers have put forward the view that
this economic deprivation has contributed to the
conflict. They would claim that cultural and
community differences are highlighted in an area
where jobs are scarce and that part of the conflict
at least is due to the destructive power of those who
have little to lose anyway. Put crudely the argument is that a man with a good job, a nice home
and a car is less likely to take up a gun than a
man who is permanently unemployed and who sees
himself as being outside the established system of
earning-power and social acceptance and who has
little chance of ever getting a job.

It is true that there is a definite class-pattern in
the kind of people who have been convicted for
crimes of violence. The majority tend to be from the
working-class and there are relatively few from the
professions. A bomber is more likely to be, for
example, an unemployed labourer than a solicitor.
On the other hand the class argument does not
explain away the loyalty to Britain that is expressed
right across the spectrum of Protestant classes.
Where else but in Northern Ireland could be seen a
working-class accordion band dedicated to a peer of
the realm? He lived in the country grandeur of an
estate nearly a hundred miles from the little
terraced homes of shipbuilders who had nothing

more in common with the object of their dedication
than loyalty to Protestantism, as understood by
Ulster Protestants.

Whatever the relative importance of religion,
culture and economics in the Northern Ireland
conflict, it is certain that the political dimension is
the tip of the ice-berg. This is the problem in its
most uncompromising form. The one million
Northern Protestants have expressed their desire to
remain British. The half-million Northern Catholics
have looked towards an all-Ireland context. So far
the British and the Ulster Protestant have failed to
work out a system in the North to satisfy everyone.
Recent events have indicated that the British
Government may be looking more to the Irish
Government to try to bring some stability to the
North, but this in itself creates the danger of a
Northern Protestant backlash in retaliation against
any attempts at a solution which would endanger
their position in the North.

Behind all these factors, including the political
dimension, lies the greatest unsolved crisis in the
North – the lack of a collective identity. The Protestant feels he is British but also Irish. The Catholic
feels he is Irish, though not quite the same as the
Southern Irish. But as yet there is no shared
Northern identity, which is to be British and Irish
in a different kind of way to the majority in Britain
and Ireland but not to feel totally British or totally
Irish. This possibility of fostering, long-term, a new
Northern identity that is acceptable to Roman Catholics and Protestants may contain the seeds of
future peace and stability.

The situation has been made infinitely more
dangerous by the deliberate use of violence. The
Provisional IRA has embarked on a campaign of

death and injury to try to make an economically harassed and post-colonial Britain tire of its Northern Irish commitment. It is perhaps less well known in the Irish Republic that the IRA's next aim is to turn on the South to force the creation of an Irish Socialist Republic, though this aim can be masked easily by an old-fashioned cry of Irish nationalism; 'A nation once again.'

The IRA violence has led, predictably, to counter-violence in the North from members of Protestant paramilitary organisations who are determined to resist an armed Republican onslaught. Horrific murders on both sides make the headlines, attitudes are hardened further, and the work of the peace-makers is all the more difficult, given that the real partition to be overcome is not the border across the island or the barriers across the community lines in Belfast, but the partition in the minds of men.

Against such a wide background of conflict and conflicting attitudes it is not difficult to understand why there is despair, particularly in Northern Ireland. One of the least hopeful signs is that many people do not have hope. They have witnessed attempts at peace-making, and these have failed. Perhaps they have tried peace-making themselves and they have been rebuffed either by the other 'tribe' or by members of their own 'tribe'. The degree of intimidation, direct and indirect, is immense. One of the worst crimes is to let the side down by breaking ranks or fraternising with the other side, however attractive that might seem. Cynics in Ireland have a saying that the man who walks in the middle of the road is liable to be knocked down by the traffic coming in opposite directions.

And yet it would be misleading to suggest that there is nothing but despair. News by its nature

tends to be reported because it is bad. And so much
of the bad news from this island has crowded out
the good news. Despite the battle-smoke, the
rumblings of war and the bitter conflicts, there is a
new stirring that seemed hardly possible in the
barren years of stagnation when both communities
and both states on this island went about their daily
business under a kind of Irish apartheid.

Just as many of the survivors of the horrific bomb-
blasts and shootings have discovered a new dimension to themselves as they passed through the valley
of the shadow of death, so too there is an awareness
among people in both communities, and in North
and South, that this drift from ignorance to a lack
of sympathy and eventually to violence must be
turned round on itself as a lesson for future generations. The lesson must be underlined as never
before that violence is not the way forward, that
there is a better way and that the ordinary people
will have to live side by side no matter who governs
this patch of earth.

Tolerance, awareness, conciliation, practical aids
to better understanding – these are at a premium
in Ireland as never before. They do not present a
soft option. One of the tragedies of peace-making is
that often the peacemakers are dismissed as naive
do-gooders. Indeed there are many peace lovers who
direct campaigns from the safety of an armchair.
There are well-meaning peace lovers who march for
peace and then go home to their tea, who watch
themselves on television and wonder why peace has
not broken out.

The reality of peace-making can be a messy business, as those close to contemporary events will
know. It requires idealism and a dash of healthy
cynicism. It requires the beauty of exposing oneself

to new ideas and it also requires the hard practical-
ities of horse-trading. Peace offers the hard option.
It is much harder to admit past wrongs, to listen
and to contribute to something new than to mouth
the old war-cries and to cloud the present with the
mindless darkness of the past.

Journalists closely involved with the peace-
makers can be much more cynical than their readers
would allow. This is a defence mechanism against
being hurt more than is bearable, by the follies of
those who mean well but who fail to detect that
noble rhetoric alone is no substitute for a sharp
political brain, realism and an ability to separate
sentiment from sense.

Fortunately there are a number of groups and
individuals who point to a better way forward. In
their actions and in their lives they have the hall-
mark of credibility. Some have come through the
unspeakable agony of having lost a loved one in the
violence, and they have emerged from the white
heat of suffering with a new vision of life that they
must share with others in order to combat violence
in all its forms.

Some people who point to the better way have not
had to pass through the wilderness leading from the
valley of death but they have observed with acute
sensitivity the need to create structures that will
relegate violence to the undergrowth of Irish
history. The contribution of these people is crucial
because they have the power to influence others in
a practical way that will make the positive approach
a credible reality and not just a pious sentiment.

The people I interviewed in the following pages
were chosen because they have something special to
say. And they ought to be heard above the din of
war. Individually they or their organisations would

not claim to have the key to the better way, but collectively they represent a mood, a stirring, a pattern that is taking shape quietly far beneath the battlesmoke. Almost undetected there is a pollen of peace spreading over so many parts of a scarred but still fertile land.

It will take time for the flowers to grow. There will be setbacks and disappointments. But the peacemakers are the people who know the power of an idea when its time has come. This is not a naive hope, but a practical and credible way of overcoming divisions and enmities.

The mood of this book is hopeful. The theme is hope from despair. The writer who has lived with all these hopes and fears, who has witnessed so much violence, who has sat in homes and hospital wards of suffering, who has seen the courage and the kindness and the humanity of so many people, who has looked back and come back from afar, who has the dash of scepticism to season any dish of optimism – this is the writer who dares to hope still and to sketch the real contributions of those who have earned the right to point to a better way forward for all.

3

No Bitterness

On 27 August, 1979, a small boat ventured forth on
the calm blue waters of Donegal Bay. It was a
beautiful morning, with the greens and the blues of
the Atlantic Ocean mirroring the clear sky and the
emerald coastline of County Sligo. The boat contained
a happy family party, with four adults (two elderly)
and three children on their way to check lobster-
pots, in the care-free atmosphere of a Bank Holiday
Monday. Within minutes there was a terrifying roar
as a bomb ripped the boat apart. It had been planted
and detonated by the Provisional IRA. Their target
was Earl Mountbatten of Burma, who had visited his
summer home in Classiebawn Castle every year for
almost 30 years. Mountbatten was a figure who had
won recognition and respect the world over, and not
least in Ireland. But the Provisional IRA felt otherwise. They murdered this man of 79 and members of
his family to show their hatred of Britain and to unify
Ireland by force.

In the explosion Lord Mountbatten died instantly.
His daughter, the then Lady Brabourne and her
husband Lord Brabourne, were badly injured. Their
son, The Hon Nicholas Knatchbull, was killed. His
twin brother Timothy was injured. They were only
14 years old. Their grandmother, Doreen, Lady
Brabourne, aged 83, died the next day. Paul Maxwell,
15, an Ulster boy who was looking after the boat, also
died in the explosion.

The Countess Mountbatten of Burma and her

husband Lord Brabourne and their son Timothy
recovered slowly from their injuries. Lady
Mountbatten now tells in an interview, for the first
time in detail, the awful events of that morning, and
its aftermath, in order to outline the lessons it may
have for others.

IT WAS a very normal morning of our annual
holidays at Classiebawn. We had been going over
there for 30 years, for a month every single summer.
It was an enormous family gathering. As I
remember, on that particular morning of 27 August
1979, we had had a family conference. I wasn't
there, because it wasn't particularly my department. My father had been getting worried about
this little boat. It had been described as a 'luxury
yacht', but it was, in fact, a 30-foot fishing boat of
the type which you see all over that part of the
world, with a little cabin, that my father had had
built locally to his specifications. The boat had a
very good engine which, however, was coming to the
end of its life. It was pretty well the last season we
were going to be able to use this boat. I have always
felt that since it was the last week of the holiday,
if the weather had turned really bad we would probably not have gone out on that day, or any more.
The engine wasn't reliable and he didn't want to
risk things for the children.

We were in a happy holiday mood. Those who
wanted to go out in the boat were getting ready, but
mercifully on that occasion our twins were the only
ones who wanted to come out with us. All the others
were doing something else. Normally many more of
the children wanted to come out, but thank God,
they didn't on that occasion. I remember very well,

sitting in the drawing-room, and waiting to go out.
I can't remember why my father was sitting with
us at that point. He was reading a book, something
like *The Last Days of Adolf Hitler*. This was rather
curious, because he normally didn't have much time
to read. He was always working at something!

We set off for the boat. My twin son Nicky, (he
was the one who was killed), was allowed to 'steer'
the car down the long 'avenue' which didn't have a
tree in sight! The group consisted of my mother-in-
law, my father, my husband, the twins Nicholas
and Timothy, Paul Maxwell and myself. Paul was a
charming boy who was running the boat for us that
year. He was very good at it, and a really nice boy.

We embarked in normal fashion, from the pier at
Mullaghmore Harbour. It was the most beautiful
day. Hot and sunny and breathless. It just couldn't
have been looking more beautiful. We sailed for
about five or ten minutes from the harbour, and we
were on our way to pick up the lobster pots, and to
have a few hours out on a lovely sunny day. I was
sitting on one side in the stern of the boat, and my
mother-in-law was on the other. She had our little
dog, a miniature long-haired dachshund, on her lap.
She was called Twiga – the Swahili word for giraffe.
She was a bit long-legged for a dachshund! She was
picked up the next day, quite unmarked but the
blast had killed her. She's buried over there, under
a little cairn at Classiebawn, with her name on a
stone and the date. That's the only memorial to
that whole occasion. A little dog's grave, just in the
corner of the castle grounds.

I remember on the boat trip that my father was
revving up the engine. My husband said, 'You are
having fun, Dickie, aren't you!' and he looked back
with a rather sheepish grin. He was such a little

boy at heart, in many ways. The last thing I
remember my mother-in-law saying was, 'Isn't it a
beautiful day!' At that moment the bomb went off.

I remember thinking afterwards, if I had been
blinded – and this was something which the doctors
had expected at one stage – that Donegal Bay in
the summer sunshine would have been a marvellous
last memory. The sea was looking glorious, blue and
green and so still and quiet. Simply wonderful. It
was the epitome of a peaceful scene. You couldn't
imagine anything horrible happening on a morning
like that.

I recall that in the boat I was reading. I used to
take with me on holidays some copies of magazines
like the *New Statesman*, which I felt I ought to be
reading up, and never had time to do at home. I was
ploughing through my *New Statesman* and I had
my eyes down. This is one reason why I had very
many scars around my eyes, and even on my eye-
lids. I remember this enormous explosion which I
thought at the time, and for several days afterwards, had been the boat's engine blowing up. I
wasn't consciously looking at anything except the
paper on my lap, but I do remember seeing the
explosion. There was a thing like a tennis-ball in
the centre and then this enormous explosion just
radiating out. I could almost see the compressed air
coming out, and then I could not remember
anything. It seemed a long, long time but it was
probably only a matter of a few minutes. The next
thing I remember was 'coming-to' in the water. I
can't remember being blown out of the boat, but I
can remember being in the water, and feeling that
I was going round and round, and over and over,
and of thinking at once of my father's description of
being sunk in HMS Kelly during the war. It was a

totally different situation but it reminded me of his
experience. He was going down at a rate of knots
into the Mediterranean – the ship had been hit by
dive bombers and had turned over at full speed. My
father was on the bridge and the Kelly turned over
with him. There was a sort of bubble underneath
and he had to dive down to get below the windscreen
that surrounded the bridge, before he could start
coming up again. He had to make himself dive
deeper. The danger was that he might swallow
water, so he put his hand over his mouth and
pinched his nostrils. Gradually he rose up and saw
it getting a bit lighter and a bit lighter, and then
he popped up on the surface, like a cork. I thought
of this story and I thought that I must do the same.
I also said to myself, 'I must tell Daddy about this
when I get back, that I remembered his story and
that I had done the same thing.' I cannot remember
hitting the surface, but I have a brief memory of
floating on the top of the water and holding on to a
piece of wood. I suppose it was a bit of the boat. I
was conscious that my face was rather a mess. I
thought that I must have hit something on the way
up. I thought 'Never mind, I am lucky that there is
something here to hang on to'. I had no idea that
the boat had disintegrated and I had a nasty fear
under the water that I was going to come up beneath
an upturned boat, and that I might be trapped, and
drown. So I was relieved that I was on the surface
and able to breathe. I remember hearing voices, and
though I couldn't take in what they were saying, I
was aware that they were agitated. They were
fishing us out of the water. Practically nothing was
left of the boat, just bits of matchwood. The only bit
of any size was the cabin and the engine, but that
sank. My poor twin son Nicky was standing either

in the cabin or in the entrance to the cabin. He may
have been trying to fetch something, because he was
a child who was always helpful. Nicholas died in
the blast, and he wasn't found for several hours. He
went down with the boat. Paul Maxwell was picked
up dead. My other twin Timothy who was sitting on
the roof was blown off, into the sea.

He had nasty injuries to the backs of his arms
and legs. He was picked up later doing a kind of
dog-paddle. My father was lifted from the water by a
young couple who were out fishing on Bank Holiday
Monday. They had also pulled us out. My husband
remembers that the girl was holding my father
upright in the water, and the one side of his face he
could see was quite untouched. I don't believe he
had injuries above his waist. He had been badly
hurt in his legs and lower body. He died instantly,
thank God. Weeks later my husband was having
nightmares and he kept saying 'I don't want to see
the other side'. He did not want to see the other
side of my father's face, in case he had been badly
disfigured. I don't think he was. The coroner said
that my father had been marvellously fit for a man
of his years. He was 79.

When my mother-in-law was picked up she wasn't
very badly hurt. She had a broken wrist and a badly
bruised back, but her face was untouched. If she
hadn't been 83 she might have survived. She had a
very robust spirit, but not a robust body. She died
mostly of shock, the next morning. But she had been
quite lucid. She had talked to the rescuers and she
had been very concerned about the children and had
spoken to my husband briefly in the hospital. I have
only one other brief memory of that day which was
that of my husband calling my name. Poor man, he
had been pulled in on top of me. He had very badly

injured legs, one so bad they thought he would lose it, but luckily he didn't. He suddenly found himself lying on me on the bottom of the boat, and he thought I was dead. He was calling my name. Luckily it just aroused me enough to make me murmur and move. I must have looked awful. My face was totally lacerated. I later had 120 stitches in it, even in my eyeballs, so I couldn't have been looking a pretty sight. I'm so thankful that I didn't have the experience of seeing anything, which my husband did. For three weeks he couldn't sleep.

I remember very briefly being in a moving ambulance, with a bell ringing. The next memory was next morning of someone in the hospital saying 'The old lady's gone'. Even in my doped state I realised this referred to my mother-in-law and that the situation was very much more serious than I had realised. If she had died it meant that everyone else was in a very dangerous situation. I thought to myself 'If she's dead, probably my father is dead too. He was young for his years, but old in age.' I was only surfacing between periods of drugged sleep. When I did come round I realised that people were talking about my husband, and about Timothy. I had absorbed the fact that Timothy was in the Intensive Care Ward with me. But nobody ever mentioned Nicky. I began to realise that if he had been alright they would have mentioned him. It's odd but I remembered Scarlett O'Hara in 'Gone with the Wind'! When she was worried about something she tended to say, 'I'm not going to worry about it now.' I said to myself 'I'm not *strong* enough to start asking questions, as to who's alive or dead. I need all my strength to get over this. I had better wait till I'm strong enough.'

I was in Intensive Care for about a week, and I

couldn't speak because I had all these tubes in me.
The only really unpleasant memory of Intensive
Care, (though, to say the least, I was uncomfort-
able!) was to do with the paralysing drugs you are
given to keep you absolutely still and to prevent
you from fighting off all the things they are doing
to you for your own good. I could not wink an eyelid
or move a finger. I remember thinking, 'This is all
very well, but if I'm lying here looking dead, at what
moment are they going to say "She's dead, switch
off the engine?"' So I thought that I must show
some signs of life, and of course I couldn't. This was
worrying, and every time I surfaced enough to be
awake I desperately tried to move something in
order to let people know that I was alive! Of course
they knew perfectly well anyway, but no-one
appreciated my worry and said, 'It's quite alright,
we know that you can't move at all'. Recently I was
asked to go to the London Medical Society to talk
about the Red Cross, and I mentioned this point to
them. It really is important to reassure someone in
Intensive Care that they are not going to switch off
the machine. I daresay there are many other people
like me who wondered how long they were going to
keep the machine running. The machine itself
makes a distinctive noise at regular intervals, and
to me it sounded as if it was saying "MUM . . . MUM
. . . MUM . . .', all the time. I knew that my twin
son was on the other side of the ward and I thought
he was calling me and I kept wanting to go to him.

On the fourth or fifth day I thought that I really
must find out what was happening. I couldn't speak,
but I indicated that I wanted to write something. I
couldn't see, and they really thought that I would
be blind, (one eye is still a bit misty). Although I
couldn't see, I wrote a sort of scrawl: 'I think Daddy

and Nicky are dead.' My poor sister didn't know what to do, whether she'd dare say 'Yes'. She said, 'I can't quite see what you've written, so I'm going to take it over to the light'. She took it to the doctor, and he said 'If she wants to know, you must tell her'. So my sister came back and she had to tell me that my father and Nicky had been killed. I am someone who always tries to look on the optimistic side. There's no optimistic side to four people being dead, but I remember thinking about Nicky, what a wonderful life he'd had as an identical twin, and maybe he would have encountered problems when he and Timothy would have been drawn apart by marriage, and he would not now encounter any of those problems. I was trying desperately to find something to balance the awful things, I suppose. It didn't work.

I was always tremendously close to my father, and I always thought that when he died it would be the most terrible moment. But I was so totally overwhelmed by the sorrow of losing Nicky that I got to the point where I began feeling guilty that I was not feeling enough sorrow about losing my father. Naturally I felt that my father had had a marvellous life. He was still well and healthy, but he was showing a few signs of getting a little older. I could say to myself, 'He will never have to face a sad, debilitating old age'. The same applied to my mother-in-law, whom I had adored. In 33 years we had never had a cross word, we were great, great friends. But Nicky, only 14 years of age, so bright and lovely, was on the threshold of life. There's nothing you can say to yourself which makes that any easier. But I suddenly thought one day, 'My poor father whom I adored—I thought it would be such a terrible thing to lose him, but the tragedy of losing Nicky at the same time has overwhelmed that other terrible loss'.

We were in hospital in Sligo for two weeks. My husband was determined to go to the funerals, in London and Kent and no one could tell him that he was simply not fit to do so. They were very wise and said, 'We'll wait and see'. There was no *way* he could have got out of bed even. He was terribly unhappy that he couldn't go to the funerals, but I was so relieved. I don't know how I would have got through them.

The people in the Sligo hospital were wonderful. There was nothing that was too much trouble. I had a badly broken leg, and I have a steel plate in my leg even now. My eardrums were gone, and I am still slightly deaf. So I'm a bit deaf, and a bit blind! The legs are fine, but I don't terribly like walking over uneven surfaces. Still, others have been so much worse. After leaving the hospital in Sligo we were taken to Belfast by helicopter and then flown to London in an aircraft of The Queen's Flight. People were very nervous for us even then, and we had a police escort at first, even in hospital. I went to Moorfields Eye Hospital, but they were satisfied that the doctors in Sligo had done a marvellous job. There was a new wing in the Sligo Hospital, which was a real bit of luck, and the doctor in charge, (a wonderful man) had been in charge of a unit in Belfast. He knew a lot about bomb injuries, and he really saved my life. They took an x-ray when I was brought in, and it was apparent that I had only half-an-hour's air left in my lungs. The lacerations were superficial, but the damage to the lungs was much more potentially lethal. I'm told the x-ray looked like that of a dead woman's lungs! My heart stopped a couple of times in Intensive Care, but I was on the machine and they kept it beating. Overall we were in hospital only five weeks, which is quite surprising. We went home with a nurse, in wheelchairs and then we were months on crutches. It's very curious but my husband and I had very similar experiences. We had almost identical injuries, both mental and physical. He lost his mother, I lost my father. We both lost our twin. We both were rather deaf. My eyes were bad, and he had such a bruised back. We both had bad legs. In many ways that has been a great help. If only one of us had been injured and the other not at all it might have been more difficult. We were able to help each other.

They were wonderful about putting us in the same ward in hospital. We were able to talk, and he and I cried equally, and a great deal. That is tremendously, tremendously important. I cried every day for perhaps six months, to a year, and intermittently for the next year. I can still cry over it very easily, after six years. Talking about the experience and the loss is of tremendous importance. I think that people who are bereaved or injured must talk, if they can. Some people feel maybe that they can't talk, because it's too painful. Yet if they can bring themselves to talk about it, I am sure that it can only be helpful to them.

Mercifully at no time did I feel bitter. Bitterness must be terrible, because it must be totally destroying. I have never felt bitter, only immensely sad. I have always felt a total horror at the acts of terrorism that are committed, particularly against families. People are shot in front of their children or wife or husband. I have a total disbelieving horror that one human being can do that to another human being.

Maybe it's because I feel that people who behave

in that way are not really human beings, in the
sense that you regard all your fellow human beings
to have essentially the same feelings. I don't know
how it happens but the terrorists seem to be sub-
human, a race apart. There was never any moment
where the idea of revenge crossed my mind. Not at
all, because if you seek revenge you only cause more
suffering.

Some of our children had sensibly asked that
instead of flowers for Nicky's funeral and my
mother-in-law's, there should be donations to the St
John's Ambulance for my mother-in-law, and to the
NSPCC for Nicky. There was a couple of thousand
pounds for him, and I asked if the money could be
used for our NSPCC work in Northern Ireland, to
provide holidays for children from both the
communities who were in need of a break. My idea
was to try to provide a point of contact between the
two communities, which is so vital if people are
going to understand one another. The fund is added
to every now and again, and is a continuing fund
called 'The Nicholas Knatchbull Fund'. It makes me
very happy to think that this money is going to
be used, hopefully, to try and create a little bit of
friendship between people over there, of both
communities.

I have not at any time felt anti-Irish. Not in any
way. What has happened has not altered my feelings. I already had this revulsion, and this total
incomprehension as to how people can behave in the
way that extremists on both sides do, so the fact
that we became victims of violence did not alter my
feelings. It just made me understand even more how
terrible it was. In the Sligo hospital they were
desperately trying to put us together again. They
felt terrible about it. The Irish nurses in hospital

over here in England told me that they felt so
ashamed and that at the beginning they didn't like
to come and nurse us because they felt so desperately ashamed at what some of their countrymen
had done. We tried to re-assure them that we loved
Ireland and that people who had done this could
not really be regarded as representatives of their
country, any more than the Bader Meinhoff
represented Germany or the terrorists in the Middle
East or Japan speak for their countries. It's the
same the world over.

I believe that people can learn from any experience, and they can learn from suffering. I think it
has sharpened my senses as to what other people
go through. You understand so very much better
because you have gone through this yourself. When
I was in hospital I remember writing letters, after
reading in the papers that something awful had
happened, particularly to mothers and their children. I couldn't bear to think of that, and I often
wrote to people who'd had such ghastly tragedies. I
had such a fellow-feeling for them.

I believe strongly in hope. If you lose hope, you
lose all desire to live. What brought me through
was the realisation that I was still alive and that I
had better get on with it, and that the family still
needed me, and that I couldn't go round moping
miserably because it wasn't fair on them. I felt
strongly that I wanted to keep alive Nicky's
memory. My father was no problem. The whole
world knew of him. But Nicholas, who was only a
child, could easily have been forgotten quite
quickly. So I have done my best to keep his memory
alive, not only through the NSPCC Fund but also
through the fund started by the Dragon School, (his
Preparatory School), and Gordonstoun (his Public

School). We gave a prize to be competed for, at
Gordonstoun, for the best example of service to the
community, and the Dragon School started its own
fund. It was nothing to do with us, and I was very
touched by it. It's a solace to think that because of
Nicky there's a little bit of good happening in the
world.

My advice to those who have been bereaved or
injured would be to talk about it, if possible. It's
enormously helpful not to shut it in. If they have
members of their family or a good friend who is able
to listen, it is extremely important to talk. Also
you've got to accept the situation. There's no point
in fighting against it, no point in saying, 'If only. . .'.
It *has* happened, and nothing is going to alter that.
You have to avoid becoming bitter, and try to think
'What's left?' and 'What can I do to be positive?'.
Also, and this is important, you must ask yourself
'What would the person you have lost really want?'
Would they want you to sit around moping miserably, feeling your life is ruined? Wouldn't that make
them much more unhappy? Wouldn't they be
pleased to find that you were going to do your best
to carry on as before, and perhaps do that little bit
extra in their memory? Perhaps try to do something
which you feel they would have wanted.

It's not easy to give advice to people. I can only say
what's been helpful to me. We have been through it
but, one reads every day of all these other terrible
things happening. Then one day it happens to you
and it makes you realise how terrible it must be for
people who have less support. We have been so lucky
in having a closely-knit and large family, who have
been quite marvellously supportive, and the number
of thoughts and messages from all over the world
has given a tremendous sense of support, to know

that other people are thinking of you. This is why I
say to anyone, 'If you hear of somebody who has lost
a person near and dear to them, do just write and
say you are thinking of them.' It's much easier to
bear if you feel that you are not alone, that others
are thinking of you. They may be far away, but you
are in their thoughts.

Before all this happened, I used to find an excuse
for not writing. I would say, 'It's too late', or 'I didn't
know them very well', or 'It will be only another
letter for them to answer'. Those excuses just don't
hold water at all. I now know what a help it is to
realise that other people have thought of you and
are continuing to think of you even much later. I
have not talked about my experiences simply
because it happened to my family, but because what
we have gone through and our experiences of
suffering might be helpful to others in similar
circumstances.

Some people might say that I appear strong, but
I've been very, very lucky in my parents. I had
wonderful parents, and a marvellous grandmother
– my father's mother – and then a supremely happy
marriage, and seven super children. I now say I
have six children here, and one in Heaven, where I
am sure Nicky is, bless him.

4

Changed by God

David 'Packie' Hamilton was a former member of two
Loyalist paramilitary organisations. He was sent to
prison twice – once for a firearms offence, and later
he was given eleven years for armed robbery. In
prison at one stage he was known as a trouble-maker.
It was during his second term in prison that he
became a committed Christian. He is now Assistant
Director of the Prison Fellowship (Northern Ireland),
a Christian organisation which helps prisoners and
former prisoners at a 'drop-in' centre in Belfast.

I WAS born in Cookstown, and moved to Belfast at
the age of ten. I lived in Rathcoole, which was
then a large housing estate several miles north of
the city. It had a mixed population of Roman Catholics and Protestants, though today it is mostly Protestant. In those days some of my friends were Catholics. I remember playing football with Bobby
Sands. He later made world headlines as the first
IRA man who died during the hunger-strikes.

When The Troubles broke out in about 1968, I
recall that the Protestants and Catholics had been
previously on good terms. We used to play truant
from school with Catholics, but when The Troubles
got bad fights broke out. Then when the paramilitaries were formed a lot of my friends were recruited
into these organisations.

One of the things which really affected me happened one Sunday when a friend of mine who was a Roman Catholic – we used to meet after chapel – said that we would have to walk home because his father had taken the car. He said that his dad was at an IRA meeting. I didn't even know what the IRA was, but years later I remembered. I went back to that chapel with a crowd of others and tried to burn it. I went down with a mob of about a hundred people, kicked the door in and wrecked it. If the police had not come we would have burned the whole place.

It was not until the early '70s that I really got involved with the paramilitaries. After that chapel incident I thought that all Roman Catholics were IRA supporters, that they were all tarred with the same brush. I was very young, I admit, but that was the one thing that triggered off that feeling. I began to hate the IRA and thought that all Roman Catholics were the same.

Yet it was not an entirely black and white situation. I remember being at a school in the area. One of our class was a Roman Catholic and some of the Protestants were going to beat him up, but I protected him.

However, in 1972 I decided to join one of the Protestant paramilitary organisations. I simply wanted to hit back. I would have been happy to have killed any IRA man, it would not have mattered so long as I knew that he was involved. The paramilitaries were looking for recruits from the local gangs, and many young people joined overnight. I was then only 16. They began to train us in the use of weapons, and mostly our operations were stealing cars for others to carry out robberies, or petrol bombings.

'But there was another reason for joining. In my mind then it showed the Roman Catholics that the Protestants were not going to lie down to the IRA.

In 1973 I was arrested, and charged with the possession of firearms, and with attempted robbery. I had been in a shop and someone saw a gun in the waist band of my jeans. I hadn't intended robbery at all. I was in there simply with a friend who was buying something. So I really felt that in the end I was sent to prison for nothing, or at least I felt I had done nothing. With all my previous convictions, I was given a five year recorded sentence and I served one year.

It was really tough inside, those were the days when the Maze was called Long Kesh. We had political status, which meant that we had special privileges. We were allowed to wear our own clothes and to group together freely. I learned more about explosives and weapon training than I had outside. It was really a school for terrorism. The day I was released from jail I decided to get more deeply involved with a paramilitary organisation. I was only 17 and I remember the advice I was given by a man inside – he said, 'Once you get out, join a paramilitary organisation and settle down'. By that he meant to go into it really seriously. It was the worst advice I was given in my whole life.

Anyway, I got involved again, but it took me almost a year to become active. Membership of this particular organisation was by invitation only. Gradually I became active, carrying out a series of robberies, stealing weapons, that kind of thing. This went on for three years until I was caught. I was apprehended only because an informer told the police and named me and several of my colleagues. So I pleaded guilty to a series of robberies. I know looking back, without a shadow of doubt, that I was also capable of killing if I had been given the opportunity to do so. I would have given more thought to getting away than about the actual killing.

In 1978 I was sentenced to eleven years, and I served five years and nine months with remission. The second time in prison was the worst. By that stage I was married, and my wife was only 18 with a young child. It made prison life a lot harder. At that time also political status was ended, so there were no special privileges. I spent 18 months in the Maze and the rest in Crumlin Road. In the Maze there were very strict conditions. The Republicans would use three wash-hand basins and toilets and we would use the next three. There was no communication between us, except through our commanders.

Remand in Crumlin Road Prison in Belfast was very tough. There were times when we fought. Even when you went to the toilet it was dangerous unless you had three or four of your mates to protect you. It was really frightening. Looking back I was crazy. I was involved in riots in the jail, and the authorities brought in the army to fire rubber bullets. Violence was a way of life, and the more I was exposed to violence the tougher I became. The turning point came one night after a snooker championship. I was in the final and I had been playing very well, and I was very happy. I went up to my cell with a book and a cup of tea. When I went in there was a Gospel tract on my bed. I crumpled it up and threw it away. It did not interest me. I saw Christianity as a weakness. But there I was sitting on the bed drinking my tea, and suddenly I thought, 'Maybe I should become a Christian!' This thought came back to me several times during the next half hour. I was trying

to think about snooker, but this thought kept
coming back to me about being a Christian. I
thought I was going out of my mind. It was only
half eight at night, yet it seemed like a nightmare.
Christianity was such a bore. I remember going to
Sunday School and the Boys' Brigade but there was
nothing real in that, nothing I could hang on to.

I began to think of my own life and thought that
there must be more to it than going in and out of
jail. I began to think of the people in my life. There
I was, aged 22, and what good had I done? It was
not a question of being afraid to go to hell. I never
doubted that there was a God, but I had no fear of
God. I knew that I would be punished and I thought,
'Well that is fair enough'. Most men in jail would
admit that they are sinners. I said to myself, 'I am
going to hell, so be it, I deserve it.' Maybe that is
why the Lord can save so many people in jail. There
is no self-righteousness about them.

'So I was lying in bed thinking through my life. I
thought about all the drinking. Drinking played a
big part. I would have drunk a bottle of vodka on
my own, although that really was just being one of
the boys. I remembered in 1972 I got shot, while up
the Shankill Road. I was taken to hospital and when
I came out of the operating theatre my mum and
dad were there. It must have broken my mother's
heart to see me like that. I realised also how
thoughtless I had been to my family. I had even told
my wife that the organisation had to come first. So
I realised, looking hard at myself, that I had failed
as a son, as a husband and as a father. There was
nothing left in my life to hang on to. Yet I wondered
still if Christ was real. As I say, I believed in God,
but I never got the point that Christ was a personal
saviour, I never realised that God would relate to

me individually as a person. It began to dawn on
me that Christ wanted my life. If He wanted my life
then why not give it to Him? So I thought, why not?
Just like that. You see, I was never an emotional
person, always pretty cool. But I thought that night,
'Maybe this is a mad notion'. I was sharing my cell
with my mate. He said to me, 'You haven't spoken
to me all night'. I said, 'I am thinking of becoming
a Christian'. At that, he went into kinks of laughter.
To be honest, I laughed too. Anyone who had known
me would have realised that I was not the type to
become a Christian. My friend said, 'Go to bed and
have a good night's sleep. You'll be alright in the
morning. The trouble with you tonight is that there
is air getting into your head!' I remember turning
over and going to sleep. It was funny, but I did not
toss and turn that night, I slept soundly.

The next morning I woke up as usual. Normally
when I woke up, the first thing I looked for was
my tobacco, and snout tin, and had a smoke. This
morning it was different, the thought came back to
me – *What are you going to do about it? Are you
going to become a Christian or not?*

By that lunch-time I had made my decision. There
was a guy who was serving twenty years for murder
and he was a Christian. I detested him for being a
Christian. He had committed murder and I knew he
was a hard man, or at least had the reputation of
being a hard man outside prison. Yet there he was
strolling around like a fairy with all these Gospel
tracts. I used to shout at him even, to embarrass
him. I used to yell, 'You can't do your time, that is
why you are a Christian'. I used to say to him,
'You're a nut', and he replied, 'Yes, maybe I am, but
I'm screwed to the right bolt!' That morning when
I was thinking about becoming a Christian he was

right in the middle of the stairway as I was walking
down. I said to him, 'I am thinking of becoming a
Christian'. He gave me a big bearhug. I was touched
by that, because he knew that I had despised him
so much. When we went out on our morning's work
he talked to me about being a Christian. The other
boys were yelling at me and making fun and they
were shouting. 'So you're thinking of joining the
God-squad!' This Christian gave me a few religious
tracts and they were very helpful. I thought about
it deeply all morning and I simply decided to become
a Christian. I remember it exactly. It was the 29th
of January 1980 at 1.30 p.m.

'That is the way I did it. I had always been like
that, very direct. Very quickly I realised I had
changed. I went to work at 2 p.m. and I met another
guy on a landing and told him that I had become a
Christian. He just laughed. One of the other guys
shouted, 'Here comes Packie the apostle!' Others
yelled, 'Don't worry he will be walking over the bath
water tonight, Hallelujah, he's seen the light.'

I was working on the same job as an IRA man
and I went to him and said, 'Paddy, I have become a
Christian'. He said, 'So what? That's your business'.
'Well,' I said, 'That's a good reason for talking if
nothing else'. After that I began to talk to him.
Some others I spoke to just scowled at me. But God
did take away all hatred from me. I had really hated
sex offenders. Nobody talks to them in prison, and
yet I was able to sit and talk with these people. That
night at tea time there were about two hundred
people in the room. Someone asked for quiet and
then said, 'Packie is going to say grace!'. I got a lot
of stick about that, but it was a good way of telling
everybody what I had done. They even began to take
bets about me. Some said I would stick it for a couple

of days, others said for a week. One mate of mine
said, 'I know you take it really seriously. I'll give
you three months!' It is important to remember,
however, that I was fully aware that the power of
Christ is the keeping force. You have to live in
constant awareness of Him and of the Holy Spirit,
otherwise you fall back. It isn't easy, although I
have said that I had made a clear decision. I am
always very aware that it is hard to be a Christian.
You always have to be on the alert and you always
have to keep close to God. Even now if I do something which I do not like, I really feel terrible but I
always have great hope because I have seen God do
so many marvellous things. It might seem odd to
say this, but I never cried tears of happiness until
I was in prison, and I really was happier in prison
than I had been on the outside.

Gradually I noticed a definite change come over
me. I no longer went around with my old mates, and
they didn't really mix with me. One former friend
cursed me up and down. He said I was a major
disappointment to him. It was quite an experience
being a Christian in prison. The people inside are
very blunt about religion. They will go to church or
Mass if they want to, but they won't go just to be
seen to be respectable. Most of them find church an
absolute bore. I think a lot of people outside who go
to church also find it a bore. But if you go to church
in prison usually it's because you have an opportunity to meet friends from other wings. It's not
because you want to worship. People often ask me,
'Did you become a Christian just to get out more
quickly?' If that principle applied, I would have
become a Christian in the dock the day I was
sentenced! There would be many others like me.
You can't get time off, you can't shorten your

remission. So even if you become a Christian or a Hindu you still serve the same sentence. There are some lifers who won't get any remission and have nothing immediate to gain by becoming Christians, but they are firm Christians. It is important, remember that. Even in prison, life is harder as a Christian. Before I was converted if anybody had tried to make a fool of me or to steal anything from me I would have tried to beat him up. But when you become a Christian you can't retaliate, because that is a very bad witness for what you believe in. Of course there is a major difference between prison and life outside. There are people outside who have their own bigotry and their own attitudes. They would not kill anybody, and they would not resort to violence, but they are often violent in their attitudes. It is important that they too remember the saving power of God.

One thing I have learned, and it is very important. There is something phenomenal happening in our prisons in Northern Ireland. I think God is using prisons in a real way, maybe even to speak to the churches outside. It seems odd that I probably get more opposition from some members of the organised churches than I did from those in prison. There are some people who ask me if I can really accept that Roman Catholics are Christians. I have no doubt that the conversions are genuine. People need to come to Christ regardless, no matter what denomination they belong to. My conversion has also had an effect on my family life. When I was in prison my wife met another man. That was very hard to take. I said, 'God, here I am trying to be a Christian and this is happening to me. What are you trying to do?' My wife and I eventually got divorced. We still have a good

relationship. There is no bitterness or hard feelings.
There was blame on both sides. I failed her, and I
left her to fend for herself. Possibly we were married
too young. She was only 17. Maybe we were both
born at the wrong time. We were just young enough
to get sucked into The Troubles. I have married
again and my wife is a Christian, and we are very
happy. Things seem to have worked out in the end.

Looking back I have many deep regrets about
what I did. Many a night I sat and cried about what
I had done. It really grieved me. I found it hard to
believe that I had done all those things. But all I
can say is that God really changed me. I now have
no hatred for anyone, I have peace. I have real hope
for Northern Ireland. God will really bring about a
change in this country. He has given definite signs
for everyone to see. If God was able to change me,
He is able change anyone. I have a firm hope for
the future and for all the people of this country. I
now work for the Prison Fellowship in Northern
Ireland. We do our best to help prisoners and ex-
prisoners and their families. I suppose when you are
put inside you really understand how others feel,
and people need a lot of help. I also speak a lot in
churches, in schools and in coffee bars, to young
people. I believe that God have given me the gift to
communicate and to get a message across to young
people, and that is very important indeed. Some of
my best friends are now Roman Catholics. I also
team up with former republican prisoners and we
speak, sometimes in universities and in schools in
other parts of the United Kingdom, and in the Irish
Republic.

I suppose it is difficult at times for people to take
in what happened to me, going from one way of life
to the other. But it depends on how you look at sin.

One thing that really bugs me is the respectability of some Christians. You get Christians who go to church and would never even think of robbing a bank or doing the kind of things which I did, but they are quite prepared to fiddle their tax forms or their business accounts. As far as I am concerned you are either in the Kingdom or you are not. As Christ said, 'You're either for me or against me'. There are no neutrals.

I now firmly believe in what I am doing and I hope to continue in my work as long as I am able. I have learned a great deal since the old days. As I have said, I bitterly regret what I have done, but I marvel at the power of God and the changes He can make in a person's life. I know I am forgiven. I am sure there are many people who knew me before my conversion who can hardly believe that I am now doing this work, speaking in coffee bars, and trying to get across the message of reconciliation – with God and then each other – to all people, and especially to young people, and also helping former prisoners and ex-prisoners. But that is life. I have changed, I have never been happier, I am at peace. I have great hopes for the future of this community. There is reason to hope. I have proved that 'In God all things are possible'.

5

Light in the Darkness

Liam O'Doherty (that is not his real name) joined the
Provisional IRA and became part of an active service
unit, specialising in the use of firearms. He was
arrested after a gun-battle with the security forces
and sentenced to twelve years imprisonment. It was
a shattering experience, particularly for his young
wife who had no idea that he had been involved with
a paramilitary organisation. He served six years of
his sentence, before being released with full
remission. For the first four years of his sentence he
remained a committed terrorist, gaining support and
strength from his association with his comrades.

During the last two years in prison he became a
Christian. In an interview he now describes how he
became involved with violence, the enormous cost to
his family and to himself, and how he is re-building
his life with the help of his family and the Christians
from the Prison Fellowship, (Northern Ireland).

I DON'T want to use my real name, because my
wife is nervous. There could be repercussions
against the family. It could make life hard for me
as well. I doubt if there would be physical violence
against us, but there would be violence of a more
subtle kind where you could be frozen out in your
own community. Sticks and stones may break your
bones, but it is almost impossible to live in a

community if people freeze you out, or if they think
you have gone against them. Names can hurt you.

It isn't easy when you come out of prison because
you are between the devil and the deep blue sea.
You have to let the security forces see that you are
on the straight and narrow because you know that
you are under their watchful eye. You must keep
yourself right with your own community, and you
have to try and act normally where you don't feel
normal. It's like being in some kind of show-case.
Some people have a stereotype image of an ex-
terrorist. They think that inside yourself you will
always hate, and have contempt for authority. And
people are surprised and suspicious if you aren't. I
wouldn't worry about surprising them, but I would
worry about making them suspicious. It is possible
to live among your neighbours without any
pressure, but its your own side you have to be
watchful for. I would be more worried about some
of the misguided supporters of the Provos. I regret
that I have to remain anonymous, and I would
prefer to stand behind my own story, and with my
own name.

I was born in Northern Ireland, and I have lived
in the same town most of my life. My father was a
manual worker, and I was the middle child in a
large family. We all had a good education and went
to college. After I left school I lived in England,
where I trained in office administration, cost
analysis and computer training. When I came back
to Northern Ireland, jobs were scarce, and eventually I became self-employed, in the sales business.

Before The Troubles broke out in 1969, it was a
different world. You could have walked anywhere
in this town, but now it is split into two halves. I
became involved with the paramilitaries through a

very gradual process. It started with nothing more than mental support, and it had nothing to do with disliking Protestants. I worked and played with Protestants. My resentment started with the security forces, because I saw things that sickened me. I don't want to be beating a big stick against those guys, but I saw police beating people for what appeared to me to be no good reason, simply because they knew who they were and what area they were living in. Discrimination was very blatant, and I suffered from it myself. If you were in an area where you could not be easily identified as a Catholic or Protestant and you were stopped by a soldier, more so the police, it seemed that all they had to do was to ask your name and where you lived. As soon as your religious background became apparent from your address, their attitude changed. You were thrown up against the wall. They didn't call you 'Sir', that's for sure. They had nothing but contempt, even though you hadn't opened your mouth.

Now there is a broadening of my outlook, where I can see the two sides of the story, where I've learned to stop and to realise that there's always a flip side to the coin. I can see where those guys could easily be provoked or angered. It took quite some time to move from mental support for the paramilitaries to getting actively involved. I was in my Twenties, and it was a conscious, cool decision. I was advised not to get involved by people who were already in it. They are not stupid men and they realised that the life-expectancy could be very short. So I was advised to think a great deal about that before I committed myself. But I still went on, because at that stage I believed the only way to bring about a change, a lasting change, was through violence. The only time people took notice was when

violence was at its worst. I believed that the fighting
was necessary. It's a very silly term to talk about
'the mindless terrorists', because the majority are
far from mindless. I moved into active service and
I was prepared to do what I was told. I was married,
but I could not share anything like that with my
wife. She might have known that I was a sympath-
iser, but she would never have thought that I would
have been involved in anything violent. She was
absolutely anti-violence. It wasn't easy keeping it a
secret, but I can say with absolute certainty that
she hadn't a clue what I was up to. When I needed
excuses I used them, and I thought it through and
used an excuse that would have stood up in court.
Maybe it's like someone who has a drink problem
or who is having an affair. He has something to hide
and he finds plenty of ways to hide it.

When I moved to active support, I was involved
with training and discipline. I was well-versed in
firearms, though I wouldn't know a bomb if someone
sat it down in front of me. On the night I was
arrested there was a gun-battle with the security
forces. When I joined the organisation, I realised
that I would have to do what I was told and within
reasonable limits I would have obeyed whatever
orders I was given. I thought of my children, and
that was one of the reasons why I was fighting. I
wanted to escalate the violence, get it over with and
allow our children to grow up without the violence
hanging over them. A united Ireland was not my
main driving force. Looking back, it was simplistic
but the main driving force was to change society
around me. When I was in prison I met people who
were well steeped in their history and culture, and
they had it all thought out, even the future. I wasn't
familiar with history, I didn't have all the answers.

I just knew where my vision began and ended. I would have supported a united Ireland, but I would not have fought for that alone.

On the night I was arrested we were moving firearms material. We were ambushed. There was a lot of shooting, but no-one was killed. I was captured and taken in, and that was when my wife found out. She was stunned. I remember seeing her and she was too shocked to communicate with me. She was sure that I had been the victim of something. I had to tell her, and I told her the truth. That was very hard. She took it very quietly, but later she started to comment and to question me. If I had killed or injured anyone she might well have left me. I had known that her reaction would have been strongly against violence, but she really did lay down the law then. It was stronger than even I had expected. Thank God, she decided to stick by me.

'Yet I still felt part of the organisation. That commitment carried me through the shock of being caught, of being imprisoned, and the de-humanising effect that gaol has on you. It was a bit like schizophrenia, having two lives to lead, being married to a girl who was totally anti-violence and yet belonging to the organisation.

I was given a twelve year sentence, even though it was my first offence. In the beginning I thought that I might even have got off because I didn't break under questioning, I didn't sign any statements. As the trial progressed, I realised that I was going down and my lawyer warned me it might even be fourteen years. You can't prepare yourself for a sentence. When the judge pronounces the sentence, it is a real shock even though you don't show it. I can still remember standing in the dock and the 'screw' next to me with his face literally inches from mine. He

was staring at me to see what my reaction would
be. I remember setting my face to appear as stony
as I could and trying not even to blink. But I
remember the sickening feeling when the judge said
'Twelve years'. It was very hard not to show any
emotion.

My wife was in the gallery, and she was tearful.
I don't know how she survived. She was convinced
that I would be coming home, so it was a double
shock when I was given what is a fairly long
sentence. She was worse off than me. She did not
see how such an upheaval could occur in our lives.
She must have found it very hard to accept, because
she did not have any commitment to the 'cause', if
you could call it that. We had a brief visit on the
day I was sentenced. This 'Committal visit' must be
the most painful of all. Even though I was shattered,
it was a great comfort and a great strength that she
did not suggest that we should go our separate ways.
She made no mention that it would be too long for
her to wait.

The remand period was the most unsettling time.
You didn't know what was going to happen during
that eighteen months. There were all kinds of prison
protests, and I was deeply involved. I would have
been regarded in prison as one of the hard-core,
though not so much as a hard man. Without a doubt
it was a school for terrorism, but we did not have
much time to learn more about weaponry or explosives, because we spent most of our waking hours on
working our ways to further our prison protests, to
disrupt the system and to see what damage we could
do. There was a feeling of being one of the boys, and
the boys were all you had to turn to in there. If
you were on your own, you were in trouble. Your
commitment helped to give you a sense of belonging.

I was inside for just over six years. Initially every day made me more bitter. In Belfast Prison the conditions were pretty bad, although some of it was self-imposed through the protest. The experience made me far more bitter. My wife visited me faithfully and stood by me, thank God. Three times a week during the eighteen months on remand, and she never missed a visit. I could see the strain she was under, and yet she kept up her own job and supported herself and the family. She never had any dole money, sickness benefit or anything like that. It's a tremendous credit to her, all that she did. Had the roles been reversed I could never have coped in the same way.

In the Prison there was a gradual personal conversion, roughly over the last two years of my sentence. The protests had been never-ending, and some of these were pretty brutal – guys being scalded and beaten. There was an ever present tension, which was hard to carry, along with the strain of just being inside. You always had to keep watching over your shoulder. All this was wearing on, and I began to see the futility. I met a lot of friends from the Loyalist paramilitaries, guys that I still know and contact. Eventually the most important part began to happen.

That was in Magilligan Prison, near Derry. I came in contact with a guy called Dr Bill Holley. We always called him 'The Doc'. He was the senior medical officer, and at that time he was the only doctor in the camp. His interest with the men inside did not end with their physical well-being. As I learned later on, he was interested in you as a person and as a son of God. That may sound a strange thing for me to say, knowing what had gone on earlier. It surprised and shocked me too. It made

me laugh at times, it made me sit back and wonder
if my time inside had made me loop the loop. Had
the four grey walls got to me that badly? But thank
God I began to see the change that was necessary.
Some people believe that prisoners who become
converted are simply looking for a way out. The only
thing I can say to that is the fact that my conversion
came during the latter part of my sentence. I was
on the 'home straight', and there was no way that
I was getting out one minute earlier than I was
supposed to. I had nothing to gain in terms of
reducing my sentence by coming to God.

Bill Holley started a Bible study. It was inter-
denominational. Some of the guys I knew well had
a great interest in this, but I was more than a little
sceptical. I thought that it was a bit of a joke, that
some of these guys had flipped. There were some
very hardline Provos, some very hardline Loyalists,
and others as well. I could not figure out what these
guys were at. I thought it was just a phase, a fad
that they would get over. One guy encouraged me
to go out, to find out what these Bible studies were
like. Previously I would have been a Sunday Christian, going to Mass and taking the Sacraments regularly, even when I was involved in violence. I
believed that the fight was justifiable. We used to
talk among ourselves and we used to say, 'If Christ
were alive He would be saying "Stop this discrimination".' We were only justifying ourselves. I wasn't
a thinking Christian.

Anyhow, I went to the Bible study as a sort of a
joke. But the feeling there was much too real, there
was a warmth in the place. I had to give respect
where respect was due. That surprised me, giving
that little bit of respect. I went a few times, and I
started to question myself. Outside the Bible study

I met Doc Holley during his normal rounds, and the interest and the concern he had were outstanding. No-one else in the system had that degree of concern for you. He was so well-placed, a man of authority, he had lots to do, lots of responsibilities, and yet he found time to stop and to find out if he could brighten your day. He would do anything for you, and you really believed that his interest in you was genuine. You could see it, you could feel it.

With the help of one guy in particular, who had encouraged me from the very start to go out to the Bible study, I started to read my Bible. At first it was like reading a novel, more an intellectual exercise than anything else. Eventually I prayed one night, really, really hard. It was one of the deepest feelings of prayer that I've ever had. I begged the Holy Spirit to open my eyes, and to give me something from the Bible to show that it was alive. When I opened my Bible it brought me to a chapter in Hebrews, it was telling me that Jesus was glad to call me his brother. Earlier I had prayed and had called Jesus my brother, and then I felt that I was not fit to do that, but this passage of Scripture completely hit the nail on the head. As I read on, the Holy Spirit told me 'not to harden your hearts'. I thought that previously my heart must have been very hard, and very cold.

There it was in black and white. The Holy Spirit was telling me to keep my heart open. It might seem a poor explanation, but it is more meaningful to me than perhaps it can be to somebody else. It gave me a message that night, and it was a turning point.

I made a commitment to Christ and I asked Him to take control of my whole life and to guide me. My cell-mate at that time was a Christian, so that was a great advantage. My former colleagues

laughed at first. They thought I was joking, but
then they realised I was serious and they became
contemptuous. Even after my commitment, I questioned myself, but God kept me strong and kept me
going.

The prison protests were being stepped up. The
Protestants and the Catholics were not mixing. We
said 'We are Christians and this is not the way
things should be. If you are going to sit apart from
one another, we are going to sit in the middle, we
are not going to identify with either side'. So the
five of us set up a table that was completely central.
There were only five of us – three Catholics and two
Protestants sitting together as Christians, and we
invited anyone else who wished to sit with us to do
so.

One prisoner had been beaten up for fraternising
with the other side, and we thought we would be
next. There was a lot of talk about these 'Christians'. They didn't quite know what to do with us,
especially the Republican Catholic side. They
thought that if you became a Christian you were
not a Catholic any more! It took some convincing to
tell them that this was not the case. They were so
surprised when we turned up at Mass. They thought
that we had become Protestants. But they could not
bring themselves to beat us up. We were threatened
with reprisals. We weren't accepted, but we weren't
physically beaten either. There was no more a sense
of belonging, no more comrades. There were very
few friends, and the only guys who could relate to
you one hundred per cent were your fellow-Chri-
stians. We decided that the best way to set an
example was to try to pray together every day. We
tried that, but some of the 'screws' objected. They
said 'There are five of you, but there should not be

more than two to a cell. . .'. We tried to use the
hobbies room, but they chased us out of that eventually too. A lot of screws objected to Protestants and
Catholics mixing together and praying together.
Maybe some of them thought it was just another
trick. To be fair, we got support from some of the
prison officers. A small number were very
supportive. They would give us fair warning if
someone was trying to come down on us, they would
talk to us, we knew that they were praying for us,
and they tried to be that bit friendly although they
were not breaking any rules to help us. There's a
couple of screws that I'm very grateful to, simply
for their friendship.

It was harder being a Christian than it was
before. You were on your own, and there were things
which you could not do as before. When the going
got rough I often questioned myself, 'Am I doing the
right thing?' but I was never tempted to go back
into the paramilitary fold again. I would have liked
to have been one of the boys again and to have been
patted on the back, rather than scorned but not at
the price of supporting violence.

I was ashamed that I had ever been stupid enough
to support violence. I was amazed at myself. I got to
know a woman, through Prison Fellowship, whose
husband had been a policeman and he had been
shot dead. I felt a terrible guilt, even though I had
nothing to do with it. It took me a long time to
sort that out in my head. Her friendship and her
Christianity, and lack of bitterness, gave me a
guilty feeling for a long time.

As well as this I was getting to know Doc Holley,
as time went on and he was *living* Christianity.
Every day that we met him you could see Christ,
because of his genuine feeling and love for you. He

was a man you could go and talk to. He was ever
open. If you needed advice or guidance on the word
of God, Doc Holley would make sure that he had
time to talk to you, even to go down to your cell and
sit with you. It's hard for anyone outside prison to
appreciate that, but to have someone in Bill Holley's
position to come in and sit and talk in your cell,
down to your level, that was a really big deal.

Doc Holley had a horrible death, from
motor–neuron disease, the same as killed David
Niven. He came in to say 'Good-bye' to us, because
he knew what he had and he knew it was the last
time he was coming in. It was 'heavy', a few of us
cried, and I remember thinking, 'He's a man of God,
he's worked for God all his life, why is God letting
this happen to him now?' It took me quite some time
to find solace in the Bible, but God told me that His
ways are so much above our ways. When I was out
on parole and when I was released I went to visit
Doc Holley. I saw his faith, it hadn't been shaken
one iota by the disease he was suffering from. His
family hadn't been shaken. His wife Marian was
remarkable, and his son and daughter. That streng-
thened my faith and it made me more determined
to have a relationship with God that could sustain
me to go through something as horrible as they had
to go through. I still miss him a lot, because I was
counting on him for when I got out. God is always
with us, but He obviously knew that I would need
companionship, and I have received that in the help
of lots of Christians around me, through Prison
Fellowship. They were with us inside, and they
helped as best they could. During my time in prison,
no-one came to my home, outside my immediate
family. No paramilitary or anyone from political
circles ever came to offer help or support to my

family. Yet once I became involved in Prison Fellowship, the Director, James McIlroy, and his wife
looked after my family. They took them to their own
home. The children always got their Easter egg and
Christmas present from James McIlroy. That might
sound small, but you constantly worry about your
family when you are in prison, and you know that
they are lonely.

I think we have a more wholesome family life
now. I don't have the secrets and the worries that I
was hiding. I don't have the same drive for material
things, I don't go drinking, and I spend ninety-five
per cent of my spare time with my family. When I
started to re-build my business life I was working
too hard, and my spiritual life began to suffer, but
thank God I have many Christian friends who seem
to come at just the right time to keep me going.
Maybe they are sent. They remind me of what I am
neglecting, though I don't think my faith will ever
disappear. My fear is that it might not grow,
through my own weakness, but I keep praying for
strength.

From all I have experienced I think there is hope
for the community. If there can be conversions like
mine, if God can do that for the guys who are really
perpetrating the violence, if He can charge the likes
of us, what can He not do? This is grass-roots stuff
which will grow and blossom though it may not
happen to suit our time-table. It is the best and the
only alternative to violence.

I regret bitterly that I had to learn the lesson the
hard way. What can I do? It's now water under the
bridge. From every angle I regret what happened,
what it cost me, what it cost my wife, my family,
my parents, but I can't dwell on that. I try to look
forward all the time. When I was inside I could not

have believed the way things could change. I am
more at peace with myself. I think that I have
learned how to deal with the violence inside myself,
with that hatred that had built up in me. Sitting at
a road-block you feel that someone thinks you are
the scum of the earth because you are an ex-
terrorist, but you can't blame those guys. Maybe
some of their friends have been injured or murdered.
Maybe those guys need my prayers. You have to
deal with the violence in yourself before you can
deal with the violence in a community. There's a
point where there can be a breakthrough into even
the greatest unbelief. St Paul was converted. If he
can be converted, and the likes of us, whom people
call killers and 'mad dogs', then the greatest unbe-
liever of the lot can be converted. There's hope for
our community because God has not forsaken us.
Doc Holley said that the light will come out of the
blackest, blackest hole. The prisons are the darkest
of dark, but that is where the light is beginning to
shine. God is using the weak and the foolish to light
the way for the wise, and the rich and the powerful.
I hope that God will give me the grace and the
courage to make the right decisions as I go along.

6

Hylda

Dr Hylda Armstrong is a remarkable woman who has overcome great personal tragedy and has maintained a positive and creative attitude to life. Her husband died at 38 from cancer, leaving her with two young boys. A much-loved niece was killed in a motor accident and she herself was badly injured in a traffic mishap. In 1973 her elder son Sean was shot dead in Belfast by an unknown gunman. Sean carried out reconciliation work with children, and after his death Dr Armstrong became a founder member of the Harmony Community Trust which has the express aim of enabling Protestant and Roman Catholic children to get to know one another better.

Dr Armstrong is a former World President of Inner Wheel, the wives of members of Rotary International. She received an Honorary D.Litt. from the New University of Ulster for her 'services to humanity'. She also received an international peace prize from the Norwegian Red Cross 'for considerable personal effort in humanitarian and social work in accordance with the founding principles of the Red Cross'.

SEAN WAS murdered on June 30th, 1973, the very last day I was President of the Inner Wheel of Great Britain and Ireland. It's odd how these details stay in your mind. Sean and his wife Morie had just come back to Belfast from Scotland and they were living in the university area. They had

just been married a week. Morie came from Indiana
and she had gone to University in California. Sean
had gone to Queen's University in Belfast and then
he worked his way around the world. He went to
Israel, America, the Greek Islands, all around. He
was an extrovert but also a deeply caring sort of
person. It took him six years. Eventually he came
back to Ireland and many of his friends said he was
crazy to come back. But he said if everybody left
who would pick up the pieces. Someone had to do
something and not just talk about it.

He was offered a post in Ireland with International Voluntary Service and he accepted it. Sean
was not too happy with the idea of bringing children
out of Ireland. He believed that these overseas
holidays in fact unsettled some children because
they found it difficult to adjust when they got back.
His idea was to show children their own country
and in doing this to teach them to live together. He
ran a number of these work camps with a difference
but he was looking for somewhere more permanent,
as a base. The night he was shot he was preparing
to take children for a holiday in the South of Ireland.

Sean was in the flat with another man when there
was a knock on the door. There was a girl also in
the flat – Pauline lived opposite Sean and Morie
and she had brought a wedding present. When the
doorbell rang she went downstairs and when she
got to the front door a young man was standing
there. 'Does Sean Armstrong live here?' he asked.
Pauline said 'Yes', and she walked back to her own
house. The young man walked up the hall, looked
up to Sean and said 'Are you Robert Sean
Armstrong?' Sean said 'Yes'. Apparently he thought
that the man was a parent of one of the children
leaving the next morning. The fellow just pulled a

gun and shot him. He got the first bullet in the
stomach and he turned to try to get into the bath-
room, and the fellow put two more bullets in his
back. He fired another three around the door frame
and then turned and ran out. Sean died in the
hospital three hours later.

Sean had been threatened before that, though his
wife didn't know. Two weeks previously I had asked
him, knowing the places he had been working in
Belfast. He looked at me and said, 'Don't you ever
be afraid, because you know yourself how destructive fear can be. No-one is going to stop me doing
what I want to do'. That was very much Sean. No
paramilitary organisation has claimed his death.
When it happened I was in London, and the police
did a fantastic job in tracing me. I was staying with
a friend and they contacted me later that night. A
policeman told me that Sean had met with an accident, that he had been shot. It began to dawn on
me that someone might have tried to injure him.
The policeman was called from the house to take
another message and when he came back he said,
'That was a phone call from Belfast'. Everything
flashed across my mind. 'Is it all over?' I asked. He
said 'Yes. In all my years in the police I've never
had to tell anyone that. Yes, your son has died.' It
was 1.00 a.m. He said 'Is there anything I can do
for you?' I replied, 'Yes, just get me home.'

The police said they would call back to my friend's
flat to pick up my things and take me to Heathrow
airport. That was about 5.30 a.m. because the first
plane to Belfast didn't go until eight. They left me
off, and I just wanted to be on my own. I felt like
crawling into a hole. The plane was airborne for
only an hour en route to Belfast, but it seemed to
take a fortnight. I was so anxious to get back that

I felt like pushing it. At Belfast Airport I collected
my car and drove straight to Morie, who was with
friends. She was hysterical and fortunately she was
able to cry. I haven't cried for 20 years, and I can't
shed a tear at all.

I would like to be able to cry but I became frozen
inside that way when my husband Armie died. He
had cancer and didn't know, and I had to become
two people – the inside person who was like a frozen
rock and the outside person who had to get on with
life. Armie was 38, we had two young boys and he
had four weeks to live. When I saw the doctor he
confirmed what I had suspected, and nothing could
be done. I got into our car and I prayed, 'Oh, please
God just get me home.' I didn't drive that car,
someone else did. I felt two hands closing over mine,
and it was the same two hands helping me when I
was coming over from London and driving down to
see Morie.

After a while we made funeral arrangements as
best we could. Later we didn't know what to do so
I drove to that lovely little church in Hillsborough
and we just sat there. I don't know why. I know that
I can be near God walking alone with my feet in
the sand and I felt near to God in that church. I felt
in some way that we were close to Sean or he was
close to us.

I did not feel bitter. Of course I asked 'Why us,
why me?' but thought again of the sea which sweeps
in as the Atlantic just outside the door of my home.
It can be very rough, and it can be calm. There are
troughs and there are crests. I was in the trough at
that moment but I knew that I could look up and
know that something would look after me. I felt this
in the church, and all I could hope was that the

same spirit would bear up Morie, because she
seemed absolutely crushed.

It was the end of Sean's life and the end of another
chapter in my life. It was terrible, dreadful. It was
like a big hole that had been torn in my being.
People talk about the heart as a physical thing but
it was as if my whole inside had been torn out and
left exposed. There was this terrible hurt which I
couldn't explain. I felt that I needed badly some
Spiritual help to comfort Morie. I prayed 'Please
God let me channel something to her'.

The days passed. After the funeral Morie stayed
on with me. She looked miserable, but she wanted to
stay though her parents in America were distracted
about her. She wanted to continue Sean's work.
Then she began to feel physically sick and she went
to the doctor. We discovered that she was pregnant.
When she was told the tears just rolled down her
cheeks. 'Oh Hylda', she said, 'God hasn't forgotten
us after all'. She cried and cried and said 'Oh if only
Sean had known.' I said that according to my beliefs
I felt that he did know. I told Morie, 'I shall miss
you terribly but if you stay here and lose this baby
through a bomb scare or something like that I would
never forgive myself and neither would you'. So for
safety's sake she went back. And she had a gorgeous
little boy. He was christened Oen, the name that
Sean would have chosen for himself.

In a way I was left alone and I began to ask
myself, 'Can you carry on the torch that Sean was
forced to leave down?' It was up to me to do something, even a little bit because if all the little bits
are put together they will add up to something. I
felt that Sean had been doing what was right. He
hadn't been the only one and I just felt that this
lovely dream of his had to be carried on. So I became

part of a group that set up Harmony Community
Trust. The idea was to bring together children from
both sides of the community divide so that they
could try to get to know one another. We had to
raise money and to look for suitable premises.

We searched around and eventually we found the
right house, set in its own grounds near the sea in
County Down. It's called Glebe House and it had
been a rectory. The cost was £40,000 and that to us
was a massive sum. However, I have been most
fortunate in the tremendous support I've been given
by the Rotary movement and the Belfast Rotary
Club spearheaded a big drive for funds in Ireland.
So Rotary and Inner Wheel raised nearly £20,000.
Earlier we had been told that this sum would be
matched pound for pound by the Government sponsored Community Relations Commission but the
Government in Belfast was disbanded and the prov-
ince was ruled direct from Westminster. So we never
got that extra £20,000 and now we face a large
overdraft.

I cannot speak too highly of the moral and practical support from Rotary and Inner Wheel. As a
former World President of Inner Wheel I have
friends in many countries and they associate me
with the work of the Harmony Community Trust.
After Sean was murdered I had a letter from an
Inner Wheel member in Pakistan. She had read the
International Minutes and she took time to sit down
in Pakistan and write to me. It was only a thought,
but it was so important to me that there was this
link. It's like all of us – when I feel depressed I know
that someone, somewhere, is thinking about me. I
am a great believer in the power of prayer. We have
a healing prayer circle in our church and I've been
an intercessor for a long time. I really do believe

there is value in prayer. Maybe it's thought-transfer, but I believe that when I'm struggling with the hurdles someone thinks of me, I get that little push and I'm on my way again. I do the same for others and I believe it works.

So I've found the motto of Inner Wheel – 'Friendship and Service' – to be a reality in my own life. You can render a service through friendship because it is not a question of money. It is a giving of yourself, and wanting to give. It is real friendship, and not just acquaintance. The two words put the idea beautifully – 'Friendship and Service'.

In another sense our friendship and service began at Glebe House, with children from both sides of the divide. They come from all over Northern Ireland. We take a group from one area of Belfast, for example, and we include a group from a corresponding area across the divide. During the summer we take them for 10 days to Glebe House and then we have two follow-up weekends. That's important. It's important not only to make friendships but to maintain them.

We've had 40 people in the house at one time, but that's a little crowded – to say the least – and we're now finishing an extension. Normally we try to take up to about 20, and we also take mentally and physically handicapped children when the others are at school during term.

It's important that you think of Glebe House through the eyes of a child and not as a member of a committee. The child should feel at home, relaxed and happy. The discussion groups are important. And during these they might discover that Protestants and Roman Catholics have a lot in common, which they hadn't realised because of their background.

I think that this is the way forward, this is the
most sensible way to sow for a peaceful harvest. It
will take a long time but a start has to be made
somewhere. It would be easy to take a negative view
if you thought continually about what has happened
in the community and what has happened to individuals. But I try to do something positive without
putting myself forward as a do-gooder. I just feel
that there is goodness around us and that there is
a peaceful and positive way forward. We must get
ourselves tuned in to that. There is a force for good
in the world. When I hear some people being narrow
and bitter I say to myself 'Isn't it awful that they
can't feel what I'm feeling'. Maybe it is like a
waveband on a radio. It is dreadful that other people
are not aware of this fantastic spiritual power just
waiting to be harnessed.

We depend greatly on volunteer helpers. We have
two paid co-ordinators but the volunteers come from
many parts of the world through International
Voluntary Service. This is marvellous because
Northern Ireland children are meeting people from
outside. We have had volunteers from Rumania,
Yugoslavia, Nigeria, the United States and most
Scandanavian countries.

It would be lovely to say that all the children we
bring together at Glebe House do in fact meet again
after they go back to their own areas. There are
difficulties, but there are also signs that we are
having our successes. You cannot measure success
in numbers because it doesn't work that way. It only
works in the child's mind, in that you would like to
think that a child who is now nine or ten might say
one day when he's twenty 'No, I'm not going to take
up a gun. I've met people from the other community
and they don't have horns. They're just like me.'

I don't want ever to take anyone down with me
or make anyone feel down. I want at least to try to
make a person feel better. You can walk into a room
full of people and there is one abrasive person who
is sowing discord. I feel equally that a person can
try to exude goodness. Maybe it's humility. We could
all do with a bit of humility at times.

I feel that I've been blessed by this closeness to
God. The only time I get worried is when I think
He's not close to me. But it is up to me to put out
my hand, to stretch, to seek Him. Some people might
say 'Why do you believe?' or 'How do you believe?'
I do not know, certainly I find it hard to explain. I
just know there is a God because He has given me
strength, though there must be more to it than that.

Oddly enough I've never asked God to make me
well or take the pain out of my legs. I was badly
injured in a car crash and I still have great pain in
my legs. I'm in pain all the time. I know what it's
like to live with pain but I also know what it's like
to be outside my body. That might seem an odd
thing to say, but I can visualise my mind outside
my body looking on at that body in pain.

People may wonder what it feels like to die. On
two occasions I've had this wonderful experience
with many years between each. The first occurred
when I was 28, after major surgery when I developed
a blood clot in my lung. Following severe pain I
became unconscious and as I was officially 'dying',
my husband rushed to be with me at my bedside. I
didn't know that he was beside me and although he
later said he did not speak during those days he sat
beside me, yet I heard him calling my name. I was
soaring upwards through a tunnel of light – there
was no sound, just a wonderful feeling of light and
peace. I felt that my spirit had left my tortured body

below and that I was going on to something superb.
My thought was 'If only I could tell my husband to
stop calling'. I didn't want to come back yet I knew
I was leaving him and two little boys. I just wanted
to float on and on. But when I was returning to
consciousness I was aware of a shadowy figure
standing near my bed who melted away when the
hospital staff and my husband came to see me.

Years later as the result of a car crash I had
multiple injuries and spent months in hospital.
Again there was a longer period of unconsciousness,
with the same wonderful feeling of soaring upwards
through light, looking down on my broken body, yet
feeling no pain. This time I had no husband to call
me back but I knew that the boys would need me.
I had not time to die although it would have been
easier than struggling with excruciating pain, to
live. To 'almost die' has given me a depth of knowledge and it has taken away any fear of death. The
crossing over is something to look forward to, but I
still must use the gift of life that has been given to
me and use it to the best of my ability.

Life is for living and there's no point in being
bitter. I am convinced that if we can all go through
the tough experiences of life without becoming
bitter we emerge as a stronger, better person. Bitterness eats away at people. I have never felt bitter,
not even at the man who shot Sean. I don't know
that I would ever want to meet him. But I would
rather be the mother of Sean than the mother of the
man who shot him. It must be dreadful to be the
mother or the wife of someone who has done something terrible. That really is a harder cross to bear.
You can lose someone and still love them, but if my
son had been guilty of terrorism in any way I would
like to think that I would still love him. But it would

be terrible to think that a child of mine had treated another human being in that way. You know how you feel if you kill a bird or a rabbit by hitting it with your car – how would you feel if you were responsible for taking a human being out of this world?

Looking back I feel terribly glad to have known Sean as a person, as well as him being my son. I could see his faults as well as his good points, even allowing for a mother's bias. But I still see him as he really was. Just as a big oak tree that was cut down, and around the root of that tree all these little saplings are growing. He is remembered not just by his family and friends. He is remembered by some of the children who thought the world of him.

I have hope in the future. The hardest thing in life is to learn to trust absolutely in something or someone, to lie back on the waves of life and to know that they will carry you on. Maybe we all build up protective coats because we don't want to be hurt again. Maybe there's two of everybody – the person that the world sees, and the person inside. And the real 'me' inside is saying, 'Yes, there's a future for Ireland, North and South'. I may not live to see it, but we are building something for the children, perhaps my grandchildren, so that they will have a country which hopefully will have learnt its lesson even if it has had to take the hard way. The real me has implicit faith that the country is going to be better after this terrible harrowing time and that there is going to be a brighter future. I should hate to think otherwise. I firmly believe that we are in the hands of an unseen power, if we will only put out our hands for help. It is there.

7

Little by Little

The two sons of Joan Orr were abducted and murdered by unknown gunmen in or near Belfast. The bodies of Malcolm, 20, and Peter, 19, were dumped on a lonely road near the airport. Joan's first husband, Frank Orr, died five years later from cancer. Their son David was married, and lives in Belfast. For some time Joan Orr lived alone in the family home, and she worked as a messenger in the Civil Service. This chapter is based on an extended interview during the period when she lived alone.

THE BOYS left the house at twenty past eight on a beautiful summer's evening. Later on a neighbour told me that there was a phone call for Malcolm, my elder son. It was his girl-friend Rosaleen and she sounded alarmed because he had not been down to see her, although she had been expecting him. She was a Catholic and we were Protestants. It didn't make any difference to me. When I came to Belfast from Jersey all those years ago I would have married my husband whether he had been a Roman Catholic or a Protestant.

Anyway I said to Rosaleen 'Don't worry, it'll be all right!' But I said to my husband 'Those boys haven't reached their destination tonight. That's not like them'. Next thing, he put on his jacket and went out to look for them, even though he had a

heart condition and had intended to go to bed early
that night. It was then that something inside me
started to take fright.

I went with my husband because I was frightened
he would collapse. We went to Rosaleen's house,
then to the boys' friends. Even the Army started
looking around. We went to a police station and my
husband said 'I want to report my sons – they are
missing'. I thought inwardly 'This is not real, this
can't be true'. When the policeman heard their ages
he put his pen down and said 'You don't expect me
to report these boys at their age!' But Frank said
'I'm afraid, they may have been picked up by one of
the paramilitary organisations'. So the policeman
took all the details.

We came home, put some coal on the fire and
made a cup of tea. Other relatives came to our house
to see us. We waited all night. I was feeling sick,
and all I could think was 'Please God, don't let them
hurt the boys too much'. Then the dawn came and
I thought 'Somehow or other they're going to be
alright'. The ten to seven news came on, and I sat
almost with my fingers in my ears, frightened and
yet wanting to know. And there was nothing. The
ten to eight news, the same. Nothing. By this time,
with the daylight and everything, I could imagine
the boys walking in. I knew Peter would say
'Mummy did you have to make such a fuss. . . !' And
I thought 'I'll be firm with Peter, I'll just say we
love you so much, we were so worried'.

Then the half-past eleven news. The announcer
said 'In Northern Ireland the bodies of two men have
been found off the main airport road'. My husband
just shot out of his chair. I said 'Frank, that wouldn't
be anything to do with us, would it?' He said 'No'. I

said 'Surely they would have said "Young men. . ." .'
He said 'That's right'.

But we went to the police station. Frank couldn't
stand the waiting any longer. A policeman said
'There's no connection' and I thought to myself
'Thank God . . .' and then I said 'God help someone
because they are going to get awful bad news
today. . . .' We had turned to leave the police station
when the detectives called us back. They said to us
'You're going to have to be very, very brave'. They
knew.

I wanted to go to identify them, but the police
would not let me. I couldn't understand this, because
I was their mother. I walked out of there and the
sun shone so brilliantly and I thought 'They are
mad in there, if the boys were dead the sun wouldn't
be shining'.

They brought us home and we just sat and waited.
I was very stunned. A reporter came to the house
and I did not know what a television man was doing
at my door. He was very gentle and he asked for a
picture of the boys. So I went to Peter's bedroom
and looked at the bed. My mind asked 'Does this
mean he is not going to sleep in that bed any more?'
It was all so difficult to grasp. Your brain wants to
reject everything. I admired my husband greatly.
He was so frightened of reprisal killings and he said
in public 'Don't let any Catholic homes suffer for
the deaths of my sons'.

Later on my anger and frustration welled up. I
said to my husband 'Your people did that to my
sons' until one day, he said, God love him, 'Joan,
they were my sons too'. I didn't want to live, I
wanted to die. I prayed to die because in my grief I
did not know that I had even room for my husband
and my other son.

I wore black a lot. I did not fancy putting on
any colour whatsoever. One day, it was months and
months and months afterwards, we were going to
the cemetery. It was quite a nice day, and I put on
a white blouse with a black cardigan. I shall never
forget the look on my young son's face when he
saw the colour. I thought 'What am I doing to that
boy. . . .' I had reached rock bottom, and when I
thought of David and the way he had looked at me
. . . I suddenly realised that if the boys came back,
they wouldn't recognise me. I was no more like the
mother that they had known.

So I thought to myself, when you get to the very
bottom, there is only one way to go. And I vowed
that my sons would not have died in vain. So now
I live my life as if they are watching me. By the
grace of God, He allowed me to realise that life is
so precious that I'm so grateful for everything that
comes my way.

I'm so grateful for the marriage I had, for the sons
I had. I would not have wanted my life without any
of it.

So many different things have helped. The
Reverend Joseph Parker lost his son in an explosion
and that man sat at Belfast City Hall on a 24 hour
fast to provide money for disaster victims. To me
that was courage. It takes guts to do that. He
inspired me in the midst of my despair, he had
known grief and here he was trying to do something
positive. I went down to the City Hall and asked if
I could speak to him. He was very, very glad to meet
me because he had watched the news on television
and his small son Stephen, who was killed later on,
had watched my husband pleading that there should
be no revenge, and that had impressed the boy. And

he'd said to his father 'Dad, why do we always fight
in Ireland?' He died only a few weeks after our boys.

I am a member of Witness for Peace which Joe
Parker had helped to found. I am not a very good
organiser, nor am I good at pushing myself forward.
I wish that I could do that, but I do my best. Each
year Witness for Peace gives a donation to any
group or individual doing community work between
Catholics and Protestants. And in our everyday life
we try to show concern for all sides and to combat
bigotry. It's no odds to me what a person's religion
might be. I don't want to know. When I sit in church
I think that the way I feel about God may be totally
different from the way the person beside me in the
pew thinks about Him. Religion is a very personal
thing.

At first I didn't want to go out. I was so frightened
about getting hurt and didn't want to like the people
in Northern Ireland any more. But letters came in
droves. And if I did go out, people would recognise
me from being on television and they would say 'Are
you Mrs Orr . . . we are praying for you'. It was as
if the hatred I was trying to build up was not getting
a chance to grow. It was being worn down. It was
as if a wall of prayer and goodness had surrounded
me, keeping out the hatred.

I live here on my own and yet it seems at times
as if my family is around me. I try to live as if they
are still watching me. But it's hard at times. I put
on two faces – one when I go out to work and one
that is private. But I try deliberately to be helpful
to people in my little way, it makes me feel that the
goodness the boys stood for is winning. It's lonely. I
get off the bus sometimes and literally run down
the road, and then I wonder what on earth I'm
running home for, because there's nobody there.

I think that Witness for Peace is worth working
for. Each year we hold a joint ceremony at Belfast
City Hall to commemorate the dead on all sides, and
that has made a great impression. When you see a
woman crying at that service you can go over to her
and put an arm around her and you don't stop to
ask her religion. You know that she has suffered
the way you have suffered, maybe the way you still
suffer at times.

I don't think that I'm a very clever person, but
sometimes I try to put down on paper what I've felt,
in the form of a poem. In reading it back to myself
I realise that I depend very much on my faith in
God. I wrote these poems and yet it took me another
time to read them slowly to understand the depth
of that faith. I never at any time felt resentful of
God, because the night the boys died . . . that was
not God's will. That was the work of the Devil.

I don't wonder why it happened to me, rather why
it was allowed to happen to them. When I think of
that night an awful fear gets hold of me. It really
frightens me. It must have been so deliberate, to
have picked them up . . . I don't know where they
died, or what time they died at. I don't feel much
about their murderers but I'll never, never forgive
them. In any case that's God's place to forgive them.
There is no reason I will accept for their death.

There must have been a blank period, when you
get so despairing it's as if you let God slip through
your fingers. Sometimes I felt 'O ye of little faith'
must have fitted me. But when I come to my senses
the faith was there in the background. I cried so
much you would have thought there were no tears
left. Then when I lost my husband it was like slip-
ping back to square one again. When there's two of

you to face something terrible, you get some
strength from each other.

My view of God has not changed, but if anything
it has become stronger. I used to sit and pray and
ask God to let me see them for five minutes, even
for two minutes. I used to glue my eyes on that front
doorway, almost willing them to walk through. But
I very seldom dream of them, just a very odd
occasion. But one night I dreamt of them, it was so
clear and vivid. I saw both of them, and Peter did
all the talking. I said to Peter 'We just want to let
you know that we miss you so much'. He said 'Mum,
we know that'. And I said 'We only want to tell you
that we love you'. And he laughed again and he said
'But we know that'. I said 'Tell me where you are
. . .' and he said 'Oh, it's great, great . . .' and they
were gone.

I went to Peter's room and half-expected him to
be lying there, but the bed was empty, as usual. I
leaned up against the doorway and cried, with the
frustration of seeing them coming and going so
quickly. Then it dawned on me 'You prayed and
asked God to see them' . . . and you did see them,
there it is. That was God's reply. It was a real
experience, they were so real to me. The only thing
I could not understand was that Malcolm – I always
called him Junior – he never said anything. He was
there, but he did not speak.

About a year later I dreamt about Junior. I was
upstairs and as I passed his room I was standing in
his bedroom. My hands touched him, and he looked
so happy. That's why I believe my sons are in a love
far greater than I could have given them. Now I
have no sense of fear. I go up to bed alone and the
lights are out, and I feel so much safer.

I find that it is easier to pray now. There are

situations that arise in my life and I ask God to help me through. Like the day my young son got married. I prayed for the strength not to crack up that day, and I didn't. David got married two months after his father died. Within five years there had been five of us living in this house and then there was only me.

Suffering deepens you. I've learned that through the death of my boys. I've learned how very precious life is. I learned earlier in my life also about the relative value of material things. During the war I lived in Jersey which was occupied by the Germans. I know what it's like to walk into a shop with the shelves empty. The fact that our radios were taken away. It taught me to appreciate things, like having enough, like the freedom of speech and of the Press. I've known people who were sent to prison for listening to the news of their country.

Our school holidays were spent walking miles collecting firewood. Going around the countryside asking farmers if they would allow us to glean in their fields because flour on the black market was so expensive. I've known hunger and having to do without. Sometimes I used to say 'Nothing has ever happened in my life'. How wrong I was. I've learned to put material things in perspective and I have learned how life is very, very precious.

I've learned to count my blessings. If anyone said 'What would you want most in this world?' I'd want my husband and my boys all back. But that's not possible so I don't let despair get a hold of me. I just count the years that I had them. And they were lean enough years. Money was scarce, yet looking back now I was one of the richest women in the world.

I live from day to day, but I always say 'God willing'. You've got so much time to think back. If

they had gone on living, there are so many little
things I now remember which would have been
forgotten about. You exercise your brain to
remember, but I don't look back morbidly. The only
thing I regret was not having more money, it was
hard going. We could never afford to go away on
holiday as a family, all together. The boys went
away with their school, that kind of thing. We strug-
gled to make sure that they went but we didn't go
as a family.

People say that my experience has helped them,
but I can't understand why. It amazes me, but some
people said I've been an inspiration. If I am, so many
things have contributed to that. The courage I have
got from God, it's not me myself. I feel embarrassed
if people say 'You're marvellous'. I don't want to
sound boastful but I think that I have the respect
of Protestant and Roman Catholic people because I
won't allow the murder of my sons to make me
bitter. There's so many good people here. The boys
had so many friends here. When I go to church or
to work everyone is so good to me, and you cannot
return goodness with hatred or thanklessness.

I think that I've conquered hatred. I applied for a
job as a messenger in the Civil Service thinking
that I would get a quiet job looking after a number
of offices. Out of the blue I was put into the Motor
Tax office where I deal with the public every day. I
make a point of going up to people and saying 'Can
I help you?' I feel that I am winning a victory over
the murders by trying to be helpful and positive and
thoughtful everyday. Maybe these murderers don't
care but how they must laugh if they see that the
relatives who are left become as corrupted as they
are.

Sometimes if I have seen people struggling with

a heavy load in the street I go over and say 'Let me
help you', just as the boys would have done. These
are little victories and when I go to bed I prop myself
up and I think of my day, and most times I thank
God for a good day. I know what living is about now,
I really do.

(Later, as the result of a television documentary
which featured her story, Joan re-married and went
to live in England, though she hopes to return
permanently to Northern Ireland some day).

8

Fighting Back

Baroness Ewart-Biggs is the widow of the late Christopher Ewart-Biggs, the former British Ambassador to Ireland. He was killed by a terrorist landmine placed under his car outside his home near Dublin, twelve days after taking up his appointment in 1976. He married Jane sixteen years earlier and they had three children, Henrietta, Robin and Kate. Jane Ewart-Biggs was granted a peerage in 1981.

I HEARD about my husband's death from my car radio, driving between Liverpool and London. I had got to London and I phoned someone who warned me that they had heard about something happening in Dublin. So I was on my way to the Foreign Office and I thought 'I'll turn on my radio' and there was this one flash in Birdcage Walk. I'll never forget that. I remember it every time I turn down Birdcage Walk. My immediate reaction that day was of disbelief. You cannot accept the unacceptable in a second. Then I drove the car into Horse Guards Parade in a hysterical way and jumped out leaving the door open. The car park attendant came running after me and he said 'You can't leave your car here, never mind leaving it with the door open'. So I just ran to the Foreign Office but I couldn't get in. The door was shut. Eventually I got in and I realised that things were very bad, because they

were waiting for me. They said 'The Permanent
Under-Secretary is waiting to see you. I ran down
the corridor and I burst into his room, I saw his face
and I said 'Is he dead'? and he said 'Yes'. I thought
my mind was going, I could not think of any way to
keep sane. The shock to a mind is something that
you cannot do anything about. If it's the body you
can take it to hospital and have it bound up, but
the mind . . . I remember saying to him 'If you had
my mind now, what would you do?'

That was the beginning of this need to replace
unreason with reason. It became an intellectual
thing because that was the only way for my mind
to remain normal. It was an effort to have an intellectual reaction rather than an emotional one. I
wanted to bring something sane out of this act of
insanity, so it seemed the right thing to stay there
in Dublin and to make a bond with Ireland against
the enemy of reason and sanity. What brings home
the loss is the lack of a person's presence, the lack
of a contribution to the family, to your life, to other
people's lives. That's why the feeling of loss
increases.

At no point did I feel bitter about the people who
killed my husband, because at no point did I allow
them to be people. That would have gone very much
against my effort of recreation. If you have a hatred
around they become someone with two arms and a
nose and a mind. Hatred only hates itself. Ireland
is a prime example of what hatred has done. Christopher and I always had the same attitude towards
any kind of brutality, whether it was extreme
political views, or callousness, even blood sports. It
wasn't that we were pacifists but we held the same
attitude towards brutality, either physical or
mental. This is what killed him, the thing he hated

most. So I treated it as something to keep on
resisting in the best way I could. The Provisional
IRA are only one part of it. This was one particular
part I could have some power against.

I don't believe in self pity, I never did. People's
nature doesn't change, it just becomes different but
the traits become accentuated by extreme shock,
horror and sorrow. I've always been a very ener-
getic, active person, and it became very important
to go on being that, I noticed the same reaction in
my children – they did not change, but they became
more so what they were. The little one was asthmatic and became a hopeless asthmatic, but a
wonderful little character with great strength. I
believe in all the Christian ethics even though I am
an agnostic. I believe in the Christian rules that
govern the community. I don't go to church but I
can believe in other people's belief. Very often I do
things in churches. I have joined other bereaved
people in a church service and I gave the address. I
was very happy to take part. In Westminster
Cathedral they had a great ecumenical service on
St Patrick's Day when they wanted people to pause
and reflect about Northern Ireland and I took a
leading part in that, but not on a religious theme,
on one based on humanity. For me the individual
concerned is the positive force. (It was a memorial
service, not a funeral.)

The first thing I did want was to get the Memorial
Trust going. This had been started immediately
after Christopher was killed and it was designed to
finance a literary prize. We launched it in Dublin.
At the reception I had in the house after the
memorial service in St Patrick's I invited all the
Irish Government to it because I wanted to establish
this bond with Ireland. We had only been in Ireland

three weeks. We'd been in Paris before that. I also
did a television broadcast which had more effect
than I could have possibly imagined. The first
impulse was 'This awful waste of this marvellous
person, dying for nothing', so the only thing I could
think of saying from the whole destruction was to
describe what Christopher had wanted to do in
Ireland, and he hadn't had the time. He had very
definite ideas. He was very pleased to go there
because it was one of the few places where a
diplomat could contribute actively towards a
peaceful settlement. There was a definite job for a
diplomat to do. So he saw this as a marvellous way
of contributing something positive. Knowing this
and realising that his death might actually make
relations between Britain and Ireland worse, it
would have been the most terrible paradox. I wished
to say those things – that the relations would not
be damaged, which was what the IRA wanted, and
also what he had hoped to do there.

Then I was going to push off. But it did involve
me, it brought me into that whole area. I had not
thought 'I am going to spend the rest of my life
working for Ireland'. I thought that I would just try
and say this one thing. Then the whole of Ireland
wrote to me after that television broadcast, and they
went on writing for months and months and months.
They were telling me how sorry they were. One said
'You may be weeping for your lost husband but
we are weeping for our lost honour'. They were so
marvellously Irish, the emotions just poured out of
these letters from ordinary unsophisticated people.

Then I launched the Memorial Trust which took
a lot of work. Various members of the Irish Government sponsored it, and then I got it sponsored in
France and Belgium because I wanted it to be a

European thing. It was a memorial that was
fashioned to suit the man. He had believed in the
European Community and had hoped to build up
a better relationship between Britain and Ireland
within the Community.

After I had done that and got myself into a public
position it was too late to retreat from this involvement. I was a designer and I went back to the Savoy
group of hotels where I had worked before and they
said very kindly 'Obviously you need a base'. So I
worked with the department that did design and
interior decoration.

I was very, very involved in the Irish quest for
peace. There were a number of groups in Northern
Ireland and the South who believed in building for
a better future. I was taken up by this. I went on
radio and television. I was asked to speak in
different places, in England and Ireland. But with
three children there were obvious limitations in
going across to Ireland.

I've always been very very interested in communi-
cations. All those years in diplomatic life you do
talk to people a lot. If you are interested enough in
what you are communicating it does not matter to
how many people you are talking, to one or 500. So
communicating was fairly easy, though I would
work out beforehand what I was going to say.

I talked mainly to groups, and to schools. Some
times religious groups, political groups. The ignorance in England about Ireland is great and as I
think that any kind of ignorance is bad it seemed a
very useful thing to do. I am still doing the same
thing.

I also lecture for money. I belong to a lecture
agency and this is what I do instead of a full-time
job, because I couldn't look after the children during

the holidays. The agency sends me off to luncheon
groups and I offer three subjects – Ireland, or the
European Community or I talk about the diplomatic
life, and that is the one they like.

It would be very difficult to give up because it is
totally associated with the man. I now have many
friends in Ireland and I have a deep affection for
them, but I do it for Ireland because of Christopher.

I see the work as a sort of embroidery. I have
never said 'There's no solution and no hope'. I have
seen it as an area where things improve a bit. There
are different sections or different stitches where
things are getting better. Greater trust is being
built up, the efforts of the individual. It's a situation
where, if you could spot a tangible thing, we would
have found a solution. So you have to do it in
another way which is to build up a situation which
finally will make a solution possible. What I do is
not anything in itself, but it contributes to the final
material which will be a community at peace. That's
the only way you can see it.

I realised very very soon that if the unacceptable
things happened to you then you had to decide
whether to withdraw from the community or to stay
with it. A decision has to be made. Your nature
comes into it, and as I have always been a very
gregarious person, I could not possibly do without
people. I realised very soon that I would have to
become the kind of person other people wanted
because people can't go on feeling sorry for you,
they can't go on offering sympathy. You can't expect
them to. I wanted to retain their friendship and
their companionship and to at least look as if I had
gained my normal composure. I think I was right,
certainly I have not lost those friends and I have
made other new ones.

I think if I had shown despair too much they
really could not have taken it. People find their own
ways of healing but I do think that the community
can help them a lot. I certainly found that
surrounded by the Anglo-Saxons who are the most
. . . they don't like to show their emotions and if
something happens which requires an emotional
reaction they just hide from it. I call it 'a leprosy'. I
remember being treated like a leper. People would
actually cross the road rather than meet me. It
wasn't beastliness, it was just that they did not
know what to say. Christopher's death had been
such a very public thing, it made it worse for them.

I remember saying in a little church in Maidstone
that if a person has signified straight away that
they wish to retreat from the community to get
healed they are perhaps better by themselves. But
if they have signified as I did that they wish to
remain part of the community, then they must meet
people on those terms. If I wanted to talk about
Christopher I would do so, they must think of me
and not their own diffidence and inhibitions. But
this is an Anglo-Saxon thing. The English are really
terrible about it.

The community must try to respect what these
people have decided. They should also try to help in
a few practical ways. There are so many things to
do, the children to look after, and not knowing how
to mend a car or how to fill in forms. Someone to
help me mend a car or fill in forms makes all the
difference in the whole world. It's the little things
usually that drive you mad. That gets right to the
threshold of despair. If there is someone who can
relieve you from some little practical problem it just
makes an enormous difference. People tend not to

think of that. I bet they do more in Belfast. People
help each other there all the time.

They are terrific, wonderful people, and that's
another hope for the future. The requirement is so
great for people who are public-minded and they do
exist. Living here in Chelsea, the need to think of
other people in the community can be non-existent.
There is also a great need here, but in a different
way. It does not glare at you so much. The good
fortune of a place that has very apparent problems
is that people do respond to it, and think about it
in a community way rather than a very selfish way.

People in England may be uncaring because they
don't know. The minute they think of people in
Northern Ireland as people with children, with jobs,
then the attitude changes completely. Until then
they just think of Northern Ireland as a place full
of thugs.

When I went to the United States I worked out a
lecture which I used. I gave quite a lot of historical
background, trying to explain why it was different
to the rest of Europe. Then I explained what the
people in different areas wanted – in England, in
Northern Ireland. Then I talked about the friends I
have in the North and the kind of work they do.
The lecture became very very alive at that point
and people started to relate to the area when I began
to talk about 'Bridie Maguire' or some person I
knew. This is the way to get a situation, which after
all is made up of human beings, over to others.

My faith is that good triumphs, though my own
experience has not worked out that way very much.
I do need to have that faith, and therefore I build
my hope on what I know is good in Northern Ireland.
One can have faith that the positive ingredients will
win, if they are given time.

Certainly I am a less happy person. That goes
without saying. Christopher used to always talk
about 'Sod's Law'. He was terribly funny. Humour
was a really important element of his character. He
was a person of very great seriousness of purpose
but he refused to see life as a tragedy. It had to be
a comedy, with him playing a very important role
in it. He was marvellously funny and he was known
throughout the Foreign Office as the great
humourist. It was often a lugubrious humour,
against himself. Continually against himself. The
Sod's Law principle was something that he reckoned
happened quite often in his life. The Law is 'Bad
luck', dropping your bread and butter and landing
butter downwards. And then to think that the
greatest 'Sod's Law' of all time has got him. He had
so much to do and say and write . . . and he was
killed for nothing, for nothing. Who did it help?

To me this was such a totally unacceptable thing.
Even if he had been killed in a motor accident it
would have been somebody driving badly, not this
other pointless thing. The pointlessness is why I
work away so hard, it's compulsive.

I do other things too. In local politics I do quite a
few talks on the European Community, this is a
great passion. We were there at the making of
Europe, in Brussels and Paris when Britain was
becoming part of it. I do go on with so many things,
not just because of him but because we agreed on
these things, we shared an interest. Peoples' basic
characters do not change, but weaknesses or
strengths can be accentuated. My super-activeness,
my resolve to achieve something has been accentuated. It's for him as well.

I do faintly believe in after-life in that I have
noticed that if I have changed at all, I am more

intellectual than I was. I've noticed myself taking up all sorts of arguments that Christopher had, I am a more serious person. I've sort of struck up a relationship with Christopher again, which is a happy one in that I am now thinking of his mind, his wit. I don't like thinking of him as a person walking around on two legs. That's very difficult. The physical loss of a walking-around person lingers for a long time.

Reconstruction can be made through religious or human resources. I can see how someone can reconstruct something on religious grounds, prayer and that kind of thing, it's a sort of catalyst. But if you don't have that it has to be built on faith in human beings, in human terms. But the faith can be as great. It has to be a more intellectual thing. It can be as constructive to the person concerned and to the surroundings, perhaps even more so. People who are religious do sometimes tend to remain within themselves more because they get comfort. My way of getting comfort is outside myself.

I can't allow myself to think anything destructive of my make-up because it's not all that strong, despite this effort. I can't allow myself to let blame to creep in, because that would make me terribly unhappy, if I thought that someone could have avoided it, if the Government had taken more security measures. There is no point in putting blame, it would only bring on a serious depression. So I only think of definite things, of constructive and positive things. You might say that this is a form of escapism but it's much better than not. I get unexpected rewards, little bonuses. When I hear that people made some little contact with each other, or when people do something constructive, groups in England who support community work in Northern Ireland, or if the Press seems to do something constructive, I count up all these things. I really do.

9

Bearing the Cross

Mrs Maura Kiely is a housewife whose teenage son
was shot dead by an unknown gunman on the steps
of a church in Belfast. She lives with her husband
Edmund and her daughter Mary in the same house
in East Belfast where her family was reared. She now
runs the Cross Group, for others who have lost a
husband or son or relative as a result of the violence.
It meets regularly to provide support and guidance
for old and new members.

IT HAPPENED on February 9, 1975, Sunday
evening. Gerard was a first-year student at
Queen's University, studying economics and he was
almost 19. He was staying in the Queen's Halls of
Residence, though normally he came home every
weekend, and he always went back on the Sunday
evening. That particular weekend he had been
studying for an examination, so he decided to stay
on at the university. We saw him there on the
Saturday and left about 10.30 p.m. As I left him I
said 'Don't forget to go to Mass tomorrow morning'.
He followed me to the door and said 'I'll go to St.
Bridget's in the evening'. That was the first Sunday
that he did not go to church with us.

Apparently he left his room at five to seven to go
to Mass. He was dead at 7.30. Two gunmen were
waiting as the congregation filed out and they fired

into the crowd indiscriminately. The road lights had
been broken, and the grounds of the church were
completely dark. So they fired against the lights of
the church when the door was opened. Gerard was
six feet tall and he was standing on the steps of the
church. When he was hit he just fell right out. The
bullet eventually wedged itself in a sinew near his
heart. I believed later that he was meant to die. If
the bullet had gone through him he would have
lived.

We were not told about his death until 1.30 a.m.
and in many ways that was the worst part. We
had friends in that night, so we did not put on the
television. When they left, after 11.00 p.m. we got
ready for bed. My husband waited to hear the late-
night news. I had almost gone to sleep, and he
rushed into the room and said 'Where did Gerard
go to Mass?' I replied 'To St. Bridget's – why?' He
said 'Two boys were shot dead there tonight'. But I
said 'That was at 7.30. Surely we would have known
by now if it had been Gerard'. So we went to sleep.

Later we were wakened by the police and a priest
knocking at the door. At that time there were a
lot of doorstep murders and I would not allow my
husband to go near the window. At that point I
never even thought of Gerard. Eventually we had
to put the light on, and a policeman shouted 'It's
the police and we have a Roman Catholic priest
with us'. When I heard that I knew what had
happened. You could have heard my shout in the
next town.

We didn't realise then why we hadn't been told
earlier. Gerard had identification on him, but he
had one letter from me to an address in Dublin
where he had stayed while working in a summer
job. The security forces spent a long time checking

with Dublin. Eventually a Belfast priest identified him.

Afterwards we queried the whole thing. They admitted that they had made a mistake, but we dropped the case. It wasn't going to bring Gerard back. They don't make so many mistakes nowadays, but it was shattering really, terrible.

I was numbed. I nearly lost my faith. I could not understand why God had allowed such a dastardly act to take place on the threshold of His church, especially when Gerard had been performing his religious duties. I was very bitter. Easter was coming and then I began to realise ... suddenly something just hit me, that God had chosen me for some reason or another to suffer. I did not know why, but I believed that God had given me this cross and that I would have to bear it. If we were going to remain bitter we were going to destroy ourselves completely as a family. From then on I began to accept his death and it was my faith and upbringing that pulled me through. I believe in life after death and I don't feel that Gerard's life was taken away. It was only changed.

I believe in Heaven, otherwise what is the point in worrying. I know that Gerard is in Heaven because he was anointed, literally in his own blood. I had always felt that children were only loaned to us, really, and that we would be expected to hand them back to God if that was what was to be.

I was also very glad that I was Gerard's mother, and not the mother of the boy who shot him. I would hate to think that I would bring a child into the world, a young man who would take a gun and go into the grounds of a church – or anywhere – and take a human life. I don't think that I could ever reconcile myself to that.

It was nearly six months before I began to accept
the whole thing. There were six of us in my own
family, and we were very close. My brother, who is
a priest, used to phone me from Australia and say
'Maura, don't lose your faith'. The family and neighbours all stood by me. We were the only Catholics
in this Park, everyone else is a Protestant. We have
had the same neighbours for 25 years, but I doubt
if I had been living in a mainly Catholic area and
that had happened to one of my Protestant neighbours, I doubt if I would have been as brave as they
were.

They must have felt terrible to have come to me
when it was a non-Catholic who had shot Gerard.
Their attitude gave me a lot of courage to meet
other people. Also, I received numerous letters from
people all over the world. That was a great help.

But when I say that I almost lost my faith, I really
mean that. At one point I began to think that there
was no God. The week after the funeral I remember
making a cup of coffee and suddenly throwing it
over a picture of Our Lord. I was almost at the stage
where I was asking God to forgive God. I was so
angry. It is so hard to think that you can rear a
child to be a good person and to love everything,
and for God to allow that child to rise from his bed
and let him be shot by someone. The priests used to
tell me that God gave the boy a free will, and he
took up a gun. My answer was that God had also
given Gerard a free will, and his will would have
been to have lived.

I thought why me? Why not one of the older people
who were at that church service. One man was shot
and the bullet went right through his nose. He was
middle aged. He had had his life – and he lived.
Why had God allowed Gerard to die, and why had

I to suffer so? Then something told me, maybe it
was the Holy Spirit, that God had chosen me to
suffer for some reason. Look what the Virgin Mary
suffered – she witnessed her son being tortured, and
crucified. We are told in the Bible to take up the
Cross so I realised that I would have to carry it. A
peace came over me after that, and I accepted
Gerard's death. I am more at peace now.

In the early stages I was rebellious. I suppose I
was half-crazy. But what I did not do, and I am so
glad now, was to take sedatives. If I had, I might
not have recovered so quickly as I did. But I began
to think also of the good things God had done.
Although I was really angry with Him, all the time
it was as if there had been a line down the middle
– one side knew there was a God, yet at the same
time I would say 'There can't be a God who would
allow that to happen'. So it was pulling me apart.

It must have been after this numbness, and the
fierce shock, around Easter I began to think of what
God Himself has suffered, though there is no human
comparison. It was from that Easter that I began to
realise that God had given me this Cross and that
He had measured it and weighed it to make sure
that I could bear it.

Yet in the early days I could not say a prayer. I
was not as bitter against the boy who had killed
Gerard as against God for allowing it to happen. I
did not go to Confession for a long time though I
took Communion. But I began to see through the
clouds, there were some bright spots. There were so
many tragic things happening, and I began to
wonder if I was being selfish.

I thought of all the things that might have
happened. He could have been tortured, as some
people were. That would have driven me to

madness. But he might as well have been killed in
a motor accident, he never knew what hit him. At
least I had that to be thankful for.

There is something else that people might not
understand. Suppose that God had spoken to me the
night before and had said 'Either your husband or
your son is going to be shot tomorrow night and you
can choose which one will live. . . .' I would have
chosen my husband. That might seem terrible, but
I have found that the women who have lost their
husbands – with maybe six or seven children – had
no-one to lean on. But I had my Edmund, if I was
afraid at night he was there. If one of them had to
die, I was glad it was Gerard, but God must have
wanted him in an awful hurry.

I also felt that if I wanted to get to Heaven I would
need to change my ways. There was no point in me
saying the Lord's Prayer if I was not prepared to
forgive. So I don't care if they never catch the boy
who shot him. As a matter of fact I would prefer
that they didn't. The police say 'He was probably
your own son's age and he probably was given a £5
note for doing it'. So he was sent out . . . I would
hate to see him being caught and being put in prison
for thirty years and in one way to rot. But his
conscience is bound to disturb him as he gets older.
If they ever did catch him I would be prepared to
meet that boy and if he wanted to talk I would be
willing to forgive him, if he was genuinely sorry for
what he had done. But I would never forget.

When I decided that the bitterness would have to
go, something inside me kept saying 'Go and meet
someone else who has lost a son'. It was like a voice
telling me what to do. Night and day it kept at me.
At that point I met a priest, and I told him about
it. He said 'Maura, why don't you start something?'

I hadn't a clue. He offered to give me all the help he could. So I went home and thought about it, and I decided to go ahead.

It's amazing. When I look back now . . . out of evil comes good. Really and truly. We were given a house to hold our meeting. So I began to compile a list of names and addresses, out of newspapers and the like. That first night we had thirty people. It was marvellous but it was also a mistake because we had too many.

When I had the list of names, I went to them personally. I did not write. I had been advised not to phone. I might have started on the wrong footing. So on the very first night I left my house with four names of people to visit. It was pelting with rain, I remember it well, I got to only one house. I arrived at 7.30 and I left at midnight. I knocked on the door and this girl appeared and I thought 'What am I going to say?' So I said, 'I am Maura Kiely and my son was shot at St. Bridget's'. And people remembered that. They remember certain incidents – the Mountbatten murder, or the Warrenpoint massacre or The Abercorn Restaurant explosion, and people remembered the boys who were shot at the church door.

So the girl invited me in. Her husband had been shot dead some years previously and she had been left with six children. So we talked together for hours. Actually I said nothing, she made a cup of coffee, and she started to tell me everything. How it had happened, how she had been told, and I could see her beginning to breathe again. She talked about her husband, about the life they had, about the children, how she was coping, or trying to cope.

I told her what we were trying to do and she said that she would be delighted to join the group. That's

what happened in every house. The next night I got
to only one house, we had so much to talk about. I
decided that I could not spend a night in every
house, so I began to phone other people and to tell
them about the group.

I can remember all those cases. How their
husband had died, how they had been told. People
were relieved to be able to talk to someone who was
not there to hear the gory details. When you have
gone through it yourself you don't want to hear
about these things. You know how that person feels.

So they all came to the first meeting. Well over
thirty. It was specifically for people who had lost
someone as a direct result of the troubles in
Northern Ireland. People go about their daily business, their family, their recreation ... and until
tragedy hits them directly they turn over the page
of the newspaper, and that's that. I would never
have dreamed of writing to anyone. Now I write or
phone as soon as it happens, or even go to them. I
found that people who came to me were a great help.

We developed into something like a support group
and we began to meet regularly. The numbers were
not big but we would organise special events –
maybe a summer picnic, or a holiday together.
There is a great need for small cell groups all over
the area but if you do not have transport that can
be very difficult. The original members of the group
were fortunate in that they had cars. Some others
were so terrified that they did not want to come out
to meetings.

Once you get too big, and once you go public you
face other difficulties. I felt that if we had gone
public too soon it would have ruined things. Eventually we decided we were ready to move more into
the public eye and to let people know that we were

in existence. We still met once a month in a reconciliation centre or occasionally in someone's house. The trouble is that if you get a large group it's more difficult to relate to one another. Ten is an ideal size.

The people went home liberated. We talked about all kinds of things – the price of meat, shopping, fashion, holidays, anything. People might think it's a morbid place but it's not. We are a shoulder to lean on. If a birthday or an anniversary comes up and someone wants to talk about their husband or relative, well they can talk about it.

Often in a tragic or violent bereavement people do not want you to mention the name of the dead person. If I mentioned Gerard's name at the start people would almost shrivel up. I could not understand why, I wanted to remember him and to share him with everyone, but people wouldn't allow you to do that. If I feel very low and I want to talk about Gerard I know that on the first Thursday of every month I can talk with the group, and no-one will mind. In fact we don't do that but we know that the possibility is there if we feel the need.

We could meet regularly for four months, and not once would anyone mention a dead relative. It is just like being invited out to someone's house for an evening meal – what would *you* talk about? You do find that mothers with children can really help one another. If you are without a father in the home and you have several teenagers, you can relate to one another in many ways. It's definitely not a morbid thing.

It's a liberation. If you really want to talk . . . if it was your husband brutally murdered and you were left with six children. And nobody, not even your family, really wants you to talk much about

that husband again, if you feel that it's annoying
them to mention the name. So you go on for months
and months, and the lump gets bigger and bigger.
Nobody will let you mention the name. Yet if I was
not able to talk about what he did, freely in the
course of conversation . . . but the public don't want
you to do that. They shrivel up. To be able to go
into a group of people who understand so well that
if you want to, you can say anything you want about
your husband or your son.. To me that's being
liberated.

It's very hurtful for people to say 'You must try
to forget all about this'. Even to put the photographs
away, to have nothing. This happens to a lot of
people. They can't come to terms with it. And they
are never allowed to mention the name, or to say
what happened.

We have policemen's wives and prison officer's
wives. The original group was more middle class.
At the beginning I said to someone we would have
the relatives of innocent victims and I was told,
'How can *you* tell who was innocent and who was
not?' Of course that was right. I should not presume
to judge anybody. The fact that someone has
committed a terrible crime does not mean that they
haven't asked God for forgiveness. There is no point
in believing in God if you don't believe in forgiveness from God. So maybe the boy who shot Gerard
has already made his peace with God.

To me it would be real reconciliation if we had a
prisoners' wives group, men serving sentences as a
result of the troubles, and relatives of those killed
in the violence. And also a group of people who have
been injured. All together at once, though how it
would work out I would not know. I think that if all

these groups came together it would be the work of God.

A priest said to me once 'The sooner you have a policeman's widow and an IRA man's widow together in the group, the better it will be'. It would be ideal but I really believe at the moment it would be too idealistic. I remember one group we tried to start, which was one hundred per cent Catholic — they did not want to talk about the weather or their children or what happened. They just tore the army and the police asunder.

There are some of our group who don't feel just as easy about the person who killed their husband or relative. One of our staunchest members, the widow of a policeman, said that if we were to invite the widow of an IRA man she would not come that night. She wouldn't leave the group, but she would not go if the other woman was there. She feels like that and I don't know if she'll ever change.

I wonder how you would get groups as polarised as that to meet, but unless you do there will never be peace. I suppose it's part of our mission to break down those barriers but it will be very long term. I doubt if a paramilitary man's widow would come — she would be prevented from doing so by intimidation. She would have to come quietly and not tell anyone.

We don't meet often enough to discuss things. Recently the widow of a prison officer said 'Why do IRA men get a Christian burial? I'm asking this because this was raised at our church last Sunday'. I said 'Others who killed were in Protestant paramilitary organisations. Do you think they shouldn't get a Christian burial?' She replied 'I've never thought of it in that way. I must go back and tell them'.

There's no point in tearing one side apart. The IRA are dreadful, they are evil, but you get the most liberal person who will tear them apart, and because the IRA are supposedly Catholic, they go on and on. Then I tell that my son was shot, and they are shocked. They have only seen the one side, but that makes them think and realise there are two sides and they start talking about the price of coal, or something else. I am not afraid to say that both sides are wrong.

I see the hand of God moving from tragedy into something creative – if you have faith that God will work and give you peace of mind after a length of time, and strength to be able to overcome that tragedy.

It's worse than knowing that a child has got leukaemia. In that case you can make a certain amount of preparation but for someone to be killed in the prime of health – even an accident or being run over by a bus is different – but in a violent death what you have to deal with is the injustice of one human being taking another human being's life.

At one point we were very worried about our daughter Mary. She was nine years younger than Gerard but they were very close. She was deeply affected by his death. She wouldn't touch his belongings, she would walk out of the house if she knew that someone was going to talk about him.

Then she became very ill and the doctor thought it was a form of meningitis. She was kept in hospital and we became worried because we thought we might lose her as well. In fact it wasn't meningitis, and the doctors never really discovered what had been wrong with her physically. Finally a lady doctor found that it had been caused by Gerard's death. She had pulled down a blind inside her.

They sent for me and asked me if she had been worrying about anything at home, and I told them all that had happened. The next day the doctor said to Mary 'That was terrible about your brother being shot dead'. She burst out in tears, and the more she cried the more they talked about it. It was like a therapy, almost the same as our group. From then on Mary was alright, it was like an answer to prayers. I often wondered how other children are, what their reaction is to the death of a father or brother or relative. What will the violence do to them?

As a family, the experience has brought us closer to God. The peace we know is the kind of peace that passes human understanding, but you still have your very low moments. Because you have walked through the winding valley of grief you don't easily forget.

My faith has deepened. I am sure of that. Once I became reconciled with God, I began to live for the time when I would see Gerard again. I would not fear death at all now because I firmly believe that Gerard is in Heaven.

10

Crime and Crisis

Ben Forde is an RUC detective working in Belfast.
He has been involved in a bomb explosion and
subjected to many dangers. Part of his job is to interview men of violence on all sides and to talk to those
who have been drawn into the web of murder and
maiming in the Northern Ireland troubles. He keeps
close contacts with people in prison and he points to
a new spiritual awakening in the unlikeliest of
places. Ben Forde has related some of his experiences
in a best-selling paperback trilogy, *Hope In Bomb
City*, *Love In Bomb City* and *Faith in Bomb City*. He
is preparing another book which will be published
shortly.

FOR THE past 26 years I've been a policeman
and for 15 of these I've been connected with the
investigation of terrorist-type crimes. My colleagues
and I have been at places where bombs were
planted, we've been blown up by bombs, we've
walked over bombs, we know what gunfire is like,
we know the whistle of a bullet. Violence is something that we've been eating, drinking and
breathing for so many years.

I've been frightened many times, and I think that
anyone who says he is not afraid is hard to understand. I've had physical fear and I still do. Everyone
in the police has a kind of death sentence hanging

over his head. I've had many friends killed, yet I go
on doing the job. At the moment I'm attached to
the RUC headquarters and I've interviewed literally
hundreds of people from all classes and backgrounds, including Loyalist paramilitaries, Republican paramilitaries, part-time soldiers, the lot.

There are times when I've wanted to run away
from the job. I've seen and heard so much and I've
experienced so much. Sometimes the strain and
stress would get you down. I have to go into interview rooms for periods of hours. I've been in situations where the atmosphere of evil was so strong
you could almost touch it. Yet I must also say that
I'm aware of a power which comes through Christ.
This is the love of God, and the capacity of love is
greater than hatred.

Maybe I've been placed in these positions to share
with other people, to learn from them and to be
led to a better role. Naturally I've had thoughts
of retaliation on occasions. We're all human, but
experience has taught me that violence breeds violence and from a Christian point of view I do not
believe that retaliation can further the peace that
can be found in the depths of our being.

As a Christian policeman, many people accept me
in a different light. Obviously there may be people
who are reluctant to accept me, though I've not been
made aware of this. There are some who might not
find me socially acceptable because they believe that
we have different standards. That's the same kind of
problem facing a Christian journalist or a Christian
engineer or whatever. But I like to think that I get
on well with all my colleagues and there has been
no indifference or animosity expressed to me by any
member of the force.

Without being pompous or self-righteous I think

that I really do earn my wages and that the job which I do would not have been entrusted to me by my authorities had they not confidence in me. So I feel that my profession of faith in my position is a direct one and hopefully that it has been beneficial to the police force and to the community. But most of all that it is God-edifying.

The idea of writing was to share this ministry with a wider audience. At the funeral service of a colleague I recall walking behind the hearse and feeling deep down that this could have been me, but my times are in God's hand. I also wanted to write to express my faith. I've had to some degree a share of suffering and sorrow and confusion in dealing with so much violence and yet I feel that the capacity of love in God is far greater than any of the evil circumstances that have faced me.

The mental strain of the job can be considerable. I do get involved with people and it's not like working at a machine. I can feel a sense of reward but sometimes I feel a heel as well. A man may be living in a nice home where there is stability of a sort, but he has done something and his conscience won't let him rest. These people don't have to confess but they feel they have to talk about it.

A man knows that by talking he may end up in prison but he is prepared to accept that and to acknowledge that this may be God's working. In one sense I sometimes feel that a home is being broken, but I would doubt that a man like this would ever be in serious trouble again.

Some people might look on me with scepticism. They may question my faith, but let them come and stand in my shoes. I don't want to use a string of religious cliches because I'm a man faced with reality and practicality, living in a man's world. In writing the books I experienced a closeness to God. The experience was deeply moving and some people have expressed a similar viewpoint. But they have become bestsellers and have opened many doors for me. Recently in one day I turned down seven invitations to speak to different groups. I've been invited to talk to schools, and to various groups, on both sides of the religious divide and it is my hope that this work will lead to better understanding between the communities.

I believe strongly that the human spirit with God's help can overcome the violence and the tragedies. As a policeman I've been in close touch with people and their families and I know that the agony of death has brought many to a knowledge of God. I've had letters from university students who perhaps have a peculiar attitude to the police in this modern age but as a result of reading the books they've had a rethink. Copies of the books have gone to Buckingham Palace and to the Vatican and to many Government leaders. But I want them to go to the people I move amongst, the IRA and others. I know they have reached such people, even in prisons. I've had letters from paramilitaries.

I believe that there is a spiritual reawakening in the prisons. It might seem odd that this feedback is coming from a policeman, who is giving evidence in cases where men might be sentenced to life imprisonment for horrific crimes that could hardly happen in any other country. I meet them, I sit with them, I spend a long time with them and I get to know them very well. I am convinced that some have committed their life to God and that they are prepared to face a long prison sentence. These are violent men and yet the capacity of love can break into their minds.

There are so many reasons for people to become drawn into the violence – environment, history, social factors. I see them as very ordinary people just like myself, but their circumstances and philosophies have caused them to be easily led. Some of the hardest men I've met have been melted by the Gospel. I've actually witnessed this. For example I've received a letter from a man I interviewed several years ago. He was convicted for robbery with a terrorist organisation but God has changed his life even though he is serving a long sentence. Some people might not believe this and I know that one judge said publicly "Conversions don't impress me", but I know people who havecome dedicated Christians and are proving that God is working in their lives. I've had a letter from a man serving a life sentence for murder and he now talks of the peace he is experiencing in God.

In prison they're away from political influences and the continuous atmosphere of murders, retaliation and hatred. They are taking stock and they have time to find themselves. I hope that I've helped to influence some of these people and I thank God for the fruit which I've seen coming through. But we must be realistic. There is much evil still around, and understanding and reason are often absent. There are still many areas where the Spirit is not penetrating because of the force of evil, and this is a fact that we are going to have to live with. We are not going to have a heaven on earth. We're going to have trials and tribulations, trouble and unbelief but that does not mean that we must not be positive in working to fulfill the sharing the good news of Jesus Christ with the help of His spirit through our everyday lives.

As a detective if I want to find out about a

terrorist organisation I like to think that I'm experienced enough to do something about it. My job is the prevention and detection of crime. I must infiltrate the enemy to try to break the system of terrorism. To break the system of violence and terrorism you have to work from within the person. I see the only source of peace in human life to come from an inner peace, whatever the external conflict, whether it be industrial unrest in Birmingham, Manchester or London, or the colour problem in America, or whatever.

I believe that through the violence of Northern Ireland you can see God working. Some good has come, even from the deaths and tragedies affecting my own colleagues. It has come through the changed lives of people and I hope that I am a better man myself as a result. People are overcoming tragedies through the stability in their lives and this is based in Christ. He is the same yesterday, today and forever. I've failed Him, I've misunderstood Him but I'm aware of the inner power and He hasn't failed me yet.

There's been a lot of love in my life, and it hasn't all been violence. I have written another book, on the power of love, because I believe that love will triumph in the end. The bomb will not blow it out of you, the bullet will not put it through you. I experience it in my home, in friends and through many of the people who've suffered. Goodness and love come through the individual, not through a political party or a government or system. Good will triumph in the end.

Recently I visited a man in prison and he said he could hardly live in the place 'for all the religion'. In other words, religion in the prison was blossoming. The same point was made by a member of the Board of Governors of another prison, and he is very excited at what is happening. There is now a note of optimism because so much is going on. I'm an optimist. I've talked to people across the divide and I am encouraged. We must press on and be positive. Despite all the violence, the upsets, the tragedies and the troubles, positive things are happening in Northern Ireland today, and it's very exciting.

11

Co-operation North

Dr Brendan O'Regan, President and a founder member of Co-operation North is one of the most distinguished of the older generation of industrial entrepreneurs in Ireland. He is the former Chairman of the Shannon Free Airport Development Company which set new standards in international catering for air travellers. He was also Chairman of the Irish Tourist Board. For his work at Shannon and his co-ordinating work for Irish institutions engaged in helping the Third World he was awarded a Doctorate from the National University of Ireland. His work for Co-operation North is the culmination of a lifetime's ambition to improve cross-border understanding and co-operation in Ireland, North and South.

A LONG time ago I came to the conclusion that economic co-operation is an important force in trying to break down misunderstanding and to bring people closer together. There are many examples of this, notably in Europe itself where there have been many tensions, great rivalries and hatreds, and violence to a degree beyond anything we have known in Ireland. After two major world wars the Europeans found a way forward and this began with an economic concept, with different people of different viewpoints deciding that they would come closer together.

Peace-making is a very difficult task and it
requires the best possible abilities and organisation,
and long-term professional commitment. It is at
least as difficult a job in a country as promoting
industry or tourism and in Ireland it is more
important than either. Therefore peacemaking
should be given the same kind of professional attention and support from everyone who is intent on
finding a solution to wear away this long legacy of
hate and misunderstanding.

In economic life generally there are people who
have entrepreneurial flair in private enterprise and
who give a lead in setting up businesses that are
dynamic in character and extent. Similarly there
are State-sponsored bodies which can be the pace-
makers. The Irish Tourist Board, Aer Lingus the
national airline, and many others have done mighty
tasks for the State and they have done it efficiently
and in competition with the best in the world. Similarly in Northern Ireland men and women in the
public and private sector have created great enter-
prises. If we can gear ourselves on this island to
deal with these economic and business challenges
we can gear ourselves to overcome the single biggest
problem facing everyone – the creation of peace and
prosperity.

This was beginning to happen in the Sixties. I
was chairman of the Irish Tourist Board and I got
to know Northern Ireland and its people very well.
It was abundantly clear that economic co-operation
was crucial in helping to break down misunderstanding and already we had decided on ways to
promote tourism for the whole island, despite our
political differences. Then in the late Sixties the
violence broke out again and it set back a great deal
of the work that had begun. Despite the violence

and the dark days I clung to the belief that we had been doing the right thing and with other people of like mind I tried to keep this going.

Various peace groups were set up and then in the mid-Seventies these were given a boost by the prominence of the Peace People. Two Northern leaders Mairead Corrigan and Betty Williams (now Mrs Mairead Maguire and Mrs Betty Perkins) won the Nobel Peace Prize for their courageous work. There were peace marches all over Ireland. When the Southern Movement for Peace began I was closely involved and helped to organise the marches outside Dublin, and to work with other groups already in existence. These included the Glencree Reconciliation Centre, Peace Point, the Peace and Justice Commission and others.

Eventually the Southern Movement for Peace formulated a 15 point friendship programme between Northern Ireland and the Irish Republic. We found however that the organisation was not suited to this task but we helped to set in train research and out of this emerged Co-operation North. It is non-governmental and derives its funds from private industry and financial institutions. Its Council has members from industry, trade unions, banks, state-sponsored bodies, local authorities and reconciliation bodies, but the members serve as individuals and not as representatives of their own organisations.

The aim of Co-operation North is to support rather than supplant the existing avenues of contact between Northern Ireland and the Republic. It is also keen to initiate new projects. Since its establishment in 1979 it has undertaken projects, which will help to increase trade, tourism and industrial

links and to improve social and cultural exchanges
between the two parts of the island.

We have organised visits to North and South by
senior members of the media and by leaders in business, professional, cultural and reconciliation organisations. We try to encourage increased co-operation
between bodies in similar fields, including
commerce, industry and the media. We try to stress
the need for a well-planned approach to achieving
more effective co-operation over a wide field. This
involves the use of the latest management techniques and the evolution of new methods of
communication which are appropriate to the task.

It is not part of my aim to offer any political
solution to the problems on the island, Co-operation
North is non-political and non-sectarian. But I do
believe strongly, however, that we in the South can
play a major part by positive and constructive effort
in non-political areas and in a non-political spirit.
This can improve mutual understanding which in
turn can help cross-border commerce, tourism and
industrial development, voluntary and community
service and this in my opinion can only but help to
improve the quality of life of ordinary people, North
and South.

Better mutual understanding, of course, is a valu-
able end in itself. If we cannot agree politically at
least we can agree to differ. We can agree to
acknowledge the sincerity with which the other man
holds his views. We can also agree to put our own
political views to one side, however sincerely we
hold them, rather than keep them in the full glare
of the spotlight. We can examine whether we know
each other as well as we think we do, and whether
there might be ways that we could actually help one
another.

If we can get to know and understand each other better and work together to improve living standards and reduce unemployment, I am sure that the more beneficial climate must work to abolish violence and the fear and hatred on which it feeds. As one who has spent his working life in promoting tourism, industry and aviation I am convinced that given the understanding and the will and the means we can also promote co-operation in economic and social fields with great mutual advantage. This is not a pious hope – we can develop a climate North and South that will threaten no evolving aspiration and tradition. Images are potent and on this island they are too often distorted, and these distortions damage all of us. We must do all we can to substitute facts for myths.

Already our efforts in this direction are beginning to have some effect. A lot more is being written sympathetically in the Southern papers regarding the North, and in my opinion, in the Northern papers regarding the South. But it is important to stress that we in Co-operation North are not concerned about Irish unity. We are most definitely not campaigning in the unity field. But we are working for greater understanding and more active co-operation between North and South in all fields.

We believe that a true spirit of good neighbourliness through well-planned and effectively executed co-operation between Northern Ireland and the Republic of Ireland can be developed. This will serve not only to erode the basis of violence but it will also improve the image of Ireland, North and South, overseas and bring about urgently needed increases in industrial investment, tourism and employment throughout the entire island.

Some people are unduly pessimistic and look on

the dark side only. They would say that this trouble
has lasted for so long and that there is nothing that
can be done of significance to promote peace and
better mutual understanding. Well, I remember the
time when people said that Shannon airport was
finished, that the new breed of long-range jets would
make the airport obsolete as a stopping point. I was
one of those asked by the Government to prevent
this happening. It was an exciting challenge. We
succeeded by expanding greatly the range of activities including the establishment of a duty-free
airport and a wide range of imaginative tourist and
other facilities in the region. Incidentally in the
early days at Shannon we employed an imaginative
chef, Joseph Sheridan, who invented 'Irish Coffee'.

We were keen to given an Irish flavour to international cuisine and I was very conscious of presen-
tation. One lunchtime I spotted a tray of roast duck
that was being carried into the dining room and I
said 'Chef, this lacks eye appeal!' He put his hand
into a basin of red currants which were being
prepared for another dish and sprinkled them all
over the duck and he said 'It's got eye appeal now'.

I replied 'Chef, that's a flash of genius'. He was
very pleased and the next day he set before me
what appeared to be the first Irish Coffee and said
triumphantly 'How's that for eye appeal?' People
will say that others had mixed the same ingredients
before, but he was the man who first gave it 'eye
appeal' with its distinctive white collar.

This is only a sidelight but the point I am making
is that where there's a will there's a way. We had
a major challenge at Shannon to keep the airport
open and to maintain living standards in the region,
and we succeeded. We all learnt from those experiences and I believe that you do whatever you decide

provided you have strong enough convictions backed by funds and good organisation. It is not just convictions but ability as well, and we have ability on this island.

It does demand more than the latest managerial techniques, ability and conviction. It is also a question of the spirit. Mankind has triumphed over adversity since he moved out of the caves. The whole evolutionary process and the whole spiritual development has proved that man is capable of moving upwards and of overcoming great obstacles. Just look at Europe in the past few hundred years and consider the amount of warring that was going on. Despite the fact that we have a terrible armaments problem now, it does not imply that we should be pessimistic.

I am not a philosopher and I don't want to go down that road, but I believe that someday mankind will look back at the period when war was so prevalent and be astounded that we could put a man on the moon while remaining unable to put together the structures that would eliminate war and violence. So we have to be optimistic because that is part of the quality which has brought mankind forward. It is not naivete. You have to have faith, which is another word for optimism. Faith, hope and charity, all three. The driving force in all this is Christianity, though sometimes we are very unwilling and afraid to recognise this.

Despite the dreadfulness of much that has been happening on this island, there is a tremendous courage and determination shining through it all, particularly in Northern Ireland. This really is most evident, when you meet ordinary people who have lived through what has been a nightmare and yet who retain goodwill, forgiveness and an unbeaten

spirit. There is a quality of steadfastness, even of
stubborn steadfastness, that is evident on all sides
of the divide. It implies that there is still a very
strong and human spirit alive in Ireland, North and
South.

Like the vast majority of Southerners I abhor and
despise violence. I admire the tenacity and fortitude
with which Northerners have endured the intermi-
nable atrocities in their towns and cities. Quite
apart from the appalling damage in the North and
the human cost on which no price can be placed, we
in the South have also suffered. There has got to be
a better way. I underestimate neither the difficulties
nor the magnitude of the task, and the violence
itself makes a way forward more essential and yet
more difficult.

But there is a right and a propitious time for
every important undertaking. The shock and horror
of the past has aroused in the public mind an urgent
desire for Christian action on a bold and imaginative scale. Now we have an opportunity for a new
start, for an unprecedented enrichment of experience. It is a challenge that we cannot decline
without very serious consequences.

12

American Shamrock

Dr A. J. F. O'Reilly, the President and Chief Execu-
tive of the Heinz Company is one of the most
successful and dynamic Irishmen of his generation.
Still in his early forties, his meteoric rise as the first
non-American to hold such a major post in this large
multinational company is as legendary as his record
in sport – he represented Ireland at rugby football at
18 and went on to win 29 caps, and he also played
for the British Lions 10 times. As an Irishman Tony
O'Reilly is deeply concerned to promote peace in his
native land and he is a co-founder and the Chairman
of The Ireland Fund, which is dedicated to the
creation of the Shamrock of 'Peace, culture and
charity' in Ireland, North and South.

THE ANCESTRY of the Ireland Fund is 'born of
desperation' out of 'self defence'. The desperation
came from the fact that having gone to the United
States in 1970 and being reasonably well-known,
every visitor from Ireland, North and South, called
me when he landed in New York and asked for help.
So if it wasn't Spina Bifida from Cork or Mentally
Retarded Children from Dublin, it was the remedial
clinic from Galway or some such body. It became
very apparent to me as I handed out a range of
addresses to these groups that very soon I would be
without friends as the ceaseless interrogation of

their generosity was conducted by wave after wave
of Irish mendicants arriving on the shores of
America.

So I suggested to a friend of mine, Dan Rooney,
that we should do something along the lines of the
United Jewish Appeal or else we would be extremely
unpopular with all our constituents in the United
States. Dan Rooney is the President of a legendary
football team called the Pittsburgh Steelers who, in
the modest idiom of America, have 'World Cham-
pion' status.

The Rooney family are legends in that they are
in the racing game, but most particularly they are
the owners of the greatest franchise in American
football history. For the 26 weeks of autumn and
winter the country revolves around American football. So Dan Rooney is a leading figure in the United
States, he has Irish ancestry and he has great Irish
concern.

He and I decided in 1975 that we would form a
fund that would reflect common aims and ambitions
for the shamrock of 'Peace, culture and charity' and
that in addition we would model ourselves on the
United Jewish Appeal which is the staggeringly
successful celebration of the Jewish ethic in
America where six million Jews band themselves
together in a common bond and a common commitment to Israel, to the extent that each year they
raise approximately 400 million US dollars.

We felt that the much larger Irish American
constituency of 22 million from the two great
traditions of the Orange and the Green could
contribute much more substantially than they had
done in the past, to their common ancestry and to
Ireland, North and South.

There is hardly anyone who has not been touched

by what has been happening in the North, and sometimes in strange ways. I have noticed among many
of my friends in Northern Ireland a polarisation of
the spirit where people who previously were gay
and buoyant, uncritical and unashamedly happy to
be in the South of Ireland are now much more
critical, much more suspicious and much more
concerned about the elements of life that divide us
rather than those which bring us together.

The violence of a friend who is killed or a friend's
child who is maimed, or a friend of a friend who is
murdered or damaged — that's an obvious way in
which the trauma of growth of suspicion and
concern between many of my friends in the North
and many of their friends in the South has been
one of the most disfiguring aspects of the current
troubles.

Maybe I 'talk' a good game at the moment but I
would be interested to see what would happen to me
as a person if a beloved child was killed in a bomb
blast. I try to personalise the sufferings of others
. . . I just don't know how vengeful or not I would
be.

The trouble has touched me in a human way. I
have this strong affection for the qualities of the
Northerner. There is something about the Northerner that is essentially appealing. The lack of
humbug, the clarity, the directness. I have always
felt very much at home with Northern Ireland
people. I revel in their sense of humour. There is a
classic line from Cecil Pedlow, a Northerner who
used to play rugby with me for Ireland. I introduced
him to a friend of mine who was writing a book
about troubled Belfast, and Pedlow replied 'For your
own sake, you'd better be quick'. On another
occasion we were pulling on our Irish jerseys for an

international game, after a bad run of failures, and
he said; 'Do you know something O'Reilly, this is
the eleventh successive defeat we're about to share
together'. Who else but a Northerner would have
such a quick and lethal sense of humour?

The other dimension which makes me so
concerned about Ireland is that it is only Irish
people who will be bothered about Ireland. Despite
the trumpeting of our own importance, despite the
enormous contribution we have made to literature
and to drama, despite our own capacity for self-
popularisation, we are largely an irrelevant nation
perched on the periphery of Europe. We are unlike
the Afrikaaner who guards the sea lanes to the
Middle East or the Israeli who lives at the flashpoint
of the most combustible geo-political situation in
the world, a crossroads both theological and in terms
of energy. Ireland is geo-politically unimportant and
there will be no Nobel Prizes for Dr Kissinger or
his successors engaging in shuttle diplomacy over
Ireland.

Therefore we are cast back on the resources of our
own tribesmen throughout the world of both the
Orange and the Green tradition. We have to try to
focus their energies and creative sense of compromise which the external universe seems to flatter in
the Irishman, upon their own ancestral homeland.

We have tried in America and others have tried
with very considerable success in Canada to form
Ireland Funds which will serve as a cross-roads for
people to show their concern for this 'Shamrock of
peace, culture and charity'.

Recently in the North someone said to me 'Do you
not think that this concept is rather naive?' and I
responded by saying that it was, and that I believed
naivete is terribly important in issues of this nature.

Cynicism is a cul-de-sac in which too many Irish
people reside. To me you need the innocence of
enthusiasm, you need the naivete of knowing that
it works elsewhere, and therefore it should be
applied by people who have concern that they should
bring a restful innocence to bear upon the Irish
question, because assuredly the Irish in Ireland
itself have failed to solve it. Therefore it is legit-
imate for us to claim some authority, be it the authority of innocence and naivete, to try to make a
contribution towards a solution.

Alex de Tocqueville, as a 32 year old Frenchman
who had spent 18 months travelling around
America, talked in 1842 about the tyranny of
democracy where 51 people can hold 49 permanently in bondage. I believe that democracy is an
imperfect method of addressing the problem of
condominium or co-existence in deeply divided soci-
eties in the world – Cyprus, the Lebanon, Iran,
Canada, even Belgium, and Ireland is not unique in
this sense.

These situations require an inventiveness where
democracy becomes the handmaiden of creativity
and not the tyrant that it can be. We have to learn
some system of accommodation and compromise so
that we have more condominium on our own island.

In America a spirit of compromise is indiginous
to the system. Americans conduct a great deal of
their political process by strident over-statement.
Both sides over-state their case, the cacophany of
sound diminishes, and they reach through some
form of verbal elasticity the middle ground where
the best of both apparently contradictory points of
view appear to fuse together and form some sort of
Hegelian synthesis. In Ireland we are not interested
in synthesis. We appear to argue from absolutes,

but I think that a number of catalysts can bring these together.

Prosperity is the first one, institutional flexibility is the second. The rigidity and illiberal nature of the Southern Irish constitution is an example of the sort of inflexibility that makes the Southern Irish point of view unattractive basically and indigestible to the Northerner. The rigid adherence of the Southerner to his point of view on family law, on issues of divorce and on certain other overstatements of the Southern Irish constitution make the hardnosed Northerner believe that there is a very high quotient of hypocrisy in the Southern personality.

In America the basic rules under which people play the game of life are flexible and elastic, and the processes of compromise are indiginous to the system. In Ireland there are two garrisons glowering at one another over the pallisades of prejudice. So it seems to me that both sides have to go more than fifty per cent down the road to meet the other.

The Ireland Fund can help by fostering everything that helps to lead to greater contact and understanding, by fostering innovations like a constitutional conference where people can address the constitutional issues and question some of the household gods like democracy – is one man one vote, and 'first past the post' the right system for a deeply divided society like that of Ireland?

Unfortunately the process of peace itself is boring. Looking at the headlines of the world it's always 'Sex, Murder, Bombs' that capture most attention. Very rarely is the Boy Scout who helps the old lady across the road the figure in the headline but we are trying to do what we can in our own small way. We are small if you take the 400 million dollars

that the six million Jews give to the United Jewish
Appeal and compare it to the half-million dollars
that Irish Americans gave last year to the Ireland
Fund. But this seed-capital can be used to focus a
lot of attention, because of the kind of people who
are involved in the Fund.

Many have a high visibility in America. Dan
Rooney for example, is one of the leaders in the
world of sport. Recently in an article in Sports Illus-
trated he said that the most important activity to
him outside football is the Ireland Fund. It's incon-
ceivable that we could have purchased publicity like
that because some 35 million American people will
read the magazine.

If we can alert more and more of the Irish-Amer-
icans to Ireland we will provide ourselves with more
funds and a substantial quantity of this money will
provide opportunities where people can get together
and talk. I have an unshakeable optimism that if
you can get people to talk, even the extremists of
this world, if you can talk to them long enough you
can prove to them the inexorable fact that a society
where people can live together in peace is essentially more satisfying than a society that lives in a
state of permanent intransigence.

We are not taking a political stance because that
would be the death of the Ireland Fund. It is better
that our objectives be ambiguous, that the methods
of trying to achieve peace be as various as the
number of supporters we have.

There are various ways. I always quote T. S. Eliot.
When someone said to him 'What does "Murder in
the Cathedral" mean?' he replied 'It means what
it says'. A certain obscurantism mixed with high
idealism makes the Ireland Fund acceptable to a
great number of people who would have enormous

difficulty in subscribing to a clearly defined narrowly stated code of objectives.

On the practical level we are looking at very many applications of which fifty per cent are for peace progress and we are screening through the Irish advisory committee which represents all strands of opinion North and South.

So in summary, the background motives sprang from the realisation of our strategic irrelevance to the world, the enormous potential in the United States, the fusion of the Orange and the Green tribes in America, the capacity to generate money, to spend it in Ireland on peace, culture and charity, to show concern, and by the very act of engaging peoples' interest to help to create tourists. These create jobs, and that creates money.

The people I'm talking about are becoming increasingly curious in the United States about Ireland. We've been able to touch people and we've told them to exorcise the simplistic notions they've had about Ireland and to learn. This can be a very tedious process, because it's a rather complicated Ireland of today. I have this absolute belief that Ireland is the most marvellous product in the world to market. I'm confident of my product.

What I am trying to say is this: 'You Americans who are part of such a young nation have had the self-indulgence of 200 years of introspection and self-improvement. It is now important to look back on your roots. Alex Haley in his *Roots* kindled a flame in America and legitimised the ethnic curiosity of Americans to go and find out something about their forbears.

In a period when Americans were trying to mould a nation together the concept of looking back was regarded as un-American. But now they are confident in the uniqueness of their own society and satisifed that it is an important achievement to be an American, people can start to look with curiosity and affection at their heritage. I think that at this point in time we are at a perfect period for the receptivity of the second, third and fourth Irish-American generation to a statement from Ireland, North and South, about the needs, the aspirations and the changing face of the island. The problems of modern Ireland will fall on receptive ears if we can communicate with these people at an idealistic level. Not for money or votes or bombs or bullets but out of a love which says 'Look, it's a wondrous heritage, both the Orange and the Green, it's a beautiful island in a stage of high development, it requires your affection, your concern, your under-standing — talk to your Congressman about it, provide it with jobs if you can, go with your children or send your children over as tourists, it is some-thing that is rewarding if you're Irish-American'.

We are saying that there are no simple answers and that any influence that you can bring to bear is needed to amend and ameliorate the simplicity of what were the traditional Irish American attitudes of the Catholic and the Protestant.

It would be much more facile for me to stand up and to speak in evangelical terms about the 'romantic oppression of Ireland', about the 'blood sacrifice', about the 'blood-red earth', about 'the wine of human sacrifice', about '700 years of bitter oppression under the heel of British Imperialism', to issue guns . . . that has a simplicity and a brut-ality that is spuriously attractive and very easy to sell, but to me it's treason. I am prepared to try to expand the rather more opaque virtue of peace.

It is a treason to preach the 'blood sacrifice'

because it is a betrayal of the Christian tradition, and it is totally unChristian to seek a military solution. I believe absolutely in the process of peace and condominium on the island and in the ingenuity of the Irish people. I am as proud of the Northern Irish as the Southern Irish, and to me it is a running sore that I have to protest my identity as an Irishman through the misunderstanding that the world has of Ireland, brought about largely by the viciousness of the tribal struggle.

Those who argue the more tedious politics of peace might find that it can be difficult to attract the attention of over-worked politicians whereas a well-placed bomb can create world attention. The awesome logic of violence can create a political attentiveness and a will to find a solution which the more boring processes of peace may not achieve. Our product of peace does not sell as well, that is the problem.

But the long term is the only way we can play the game, the boring game of peace. What I am interested in is condominium, where we all live together on our own island in peace and harmony, with peculiarly Irish institutions, North and South and even, if necessary, East and West.

The greatest policymaker of all is the force of circumstances, but I believe that what I'm trying to do is baptised by its relevance. This is very important work. Yet to set a timetable is an exercise calculated to increase your ineffectiveness and your sense of frustration. Life is not like that, it is a series of random opportunities, but if the Lord ordains that I will be an instrument, primary or otherwise, in helping to change the face of modern Ireland in a peaceful way, I will try to help to bring about that

change. I've tasted other potions and they just don't
taste like Ireland.

13

Going Dutch

The Reverend Aat van Rhijn, a Presbyterian, and
Father Andre Lascaris, a Dominican, are Dutch
clerics who have been working with a Dutch-
Northern Ireland Foundation to promote better
understanding in Ulster. Both have extensive experience in adult education and they have organised
conferences, mainly in Holland, to help Northern
Ireland people to look at themselves in a new context
and to look at Ulster from a distance. The work of
the Dutch-Northern Irish Foundation is funded by
the Dutch Council of Churches as its contribution
towards trying to help in the Irish situation. Aat van
Rhijn recently left the Foundation to concentrate on
pastoral work.

AT THE start of the troubles, the Dutch Council
of Churches asked the Irish Council of Churches, 'What can we do for you'. The Irish proposed
that we organise a conference for key people in
Northern Ireland and that's how it began.

We have held nearly 20 conferences involving all
kinds of people from Northern Ireland – neighbourhood groups, mostly mixed, a great variety of
professions, social workers, politicians, Protestant
and Roman Catholic clergy, police, paramilitaries
and others. When we started we did not know
exactly how it would develop, but the original idea

was to take people out of the situation and allow
them to meet together in peace and quiet in Holland
— they could not do this back home. We also wanted
to make them look back on Northern Ireland from
a distance.

This is a method used by other groups dealing
with international conflict and we feel we are among
the more experienced people in Europe working in
this area of human relationships. The initial conference was one of the most interesting because it
became clear to us what the problems were about,
and we were very impressed by the commitment
of the people involved to try to bring about better
relationships.

Another important conference was the one
involving neighbourhood groups and this led
indirectly to a meeting between churchmen and
leading members of the Provisional IRA. The conference involving the paramilitaries on both sides was
also memorable. It began with a low profile so that
the marginal members of these groups were
approached, but in the course of organising the
conference it became more important in the eyes of
the paramilitaries themselves, and the more significant figures joined in.

The theme of the conference was the establishment of co-operatives, because the Catholics had
already established some of these in Belfast partly
to give expression to their Socialist principles and
partly to earn some money. The Protestants also
wanted to establish co-operatives to provide employment so they wanted to learn from the Catholics. In
itself it was a very emotional affair because it was
a unique occasion. We found it very difficult and yet
challenging because we had to use all our skills and
experience to make the thing work.

We found it difficult to know exactly what topics
we could safely introduce for discussion and those
which we could not. What could or could not be
brought into the formal sessions and what could be
left to the informal contacts? There was the
difficulty of allowing people the freedom of speech
and yet taking the risk that someone would say
something which would leave himself open and
isolated when he went back to Ireland. In other
words we had to try to protect some people against
themselves.

Eventually the Press heard about it and it
developed into an international 'affair' which was a
pity, because it could have been repeated. But in
itself it was an interesting experiment and a quite
successful attempt to get the paramilitaries to talk
to each other. We learned a lot, what kind of people
paramilitaries are, how they talk, how they think,
how they behave, and it provided useful background
material for other conferences.

We tried to show them that although they were
enemies they had points of common interest – unemployment, friends in prison, and coming out of
prison but having to work – it was the same problem
for the Republican or the Loyalist.

In general we have tried to do something about
the value-system of Northern Irish society, to help
people to reflect on their own values, to encourage
them to ask themselves 'What is important for me?',
or even 'What is important for the other fellow?', to
reflect on a society built on new values. We are
convinced that, although you can't measure it, this
approach has made some contribution – the fact that
people are confronted with a completely different
society for the first time, this is an eye-opener. It is
like sowing seeds but it has to be seen in context

with all the other attempts to build something
worthwhile in Northern Ireland. It may not be a
major contribution, given our resources, but we are
working in the right field and that itself is
important.

We were clear from the start that we could not
bring about peace in Northern Ireland. That has not
been our task or our aspiration. Our contribution
has been to try to show that you can deal with a
conflict in a different way – at least you can talk
about it – and secondly on a methodical level,
having opinions or views is one thing but that the
experience of life is another thing. And that you
should create the possibilities where people can
share experiences, offering them new experiences
and realising that people change by experience,
more than anything else.

As Dutchmen we believe that we are citizens of
the world in the sense that if something happens in
South Africa or the Middle East or North America
or Ireland it has something to do with us, too. Our
experience of the German occupation in the war
helped us to realise that if Germany had something
to do with our lives, so had China and all the others.
What happens in Northern Ireland has an effect
on us as we are somehow involved, and this says
something to us as human beings. Being Christians
and being clerics is an asset because people in
Northern Ireland talk about 'Protestants' and 'Catholics' and this makes it easier to move into that
situation.

We felt actively engaged and we found it very
rewarding, that we could actually do something.
There are so many situations where you feel that
you can't do this – what could you do about Afghan-
istan? Nothing, practically, but in Ireland there was

the possibility of doing something concrete. It was
not a remote Irish mess. So it all had something to
do with being human and with being convinced that
peace and justice are very important and the Scripture again and again hammers home the point
about peace, justice and non-violence, what it is to
be human, what it means to be a man.

In purely practical terms there was a request from
the European Council of Churches – can you do
something for Northern Ireland. We felt a certain
loyalty not to the Irish as such but to the Europeans
who were actually prepared to try and do something.
It was a request – the Irish thing was not our hobby
– and if this request had not come we would not
have become involved.

There was also the growing conviction that
conflict provides an opportunity for renewal. The
very first conference 'Social change and social
conflict' had a great deal of theology and Biblical
understanding in it. A conflict can be a sign that we
are preparing to enter a new future but, to pick that
up, something must change between us and within
people themselves. As people we ourselves are more
able to deal with conflict than several years ago
when we began to run these conferences.

It also means that you become aware of conflicts
elsewhere and the theme of conflicts in Scripture,
the conflicts of Jesus, the conflicts of church history.
Very often Christians have the idea that love forbids
conflict, and most have grown up with this concept.
It takes a long time to set oneself free from this, not
only intellectually, but to understand this –
emotionally and with your heart – takes a long time.

Personally we have been touched by the suffering.
At one conference there were four boys – two Catholics and two Protestants – who worked together,

and back in Ireland one of the boys was shot dead.
Another boy who was at another conference was
beaten severely by his own group when he returned
home. Another man who came to one of the conferences was murdered.

We could not fail to be touched by the lives of
many of the people who came – they told us their
stories, they talked about their hopes and their
fears. Ours was not just an intellectual involvement
– if it had been that it would not have changed us.
The past few years have played an important part
in our own lives though it is not easy to describe
exactly how. Let's say that we have grown. It has
been both a pleasure and an enrichment to meet, to
share with, to try to help and to learn from all these
people.

The Irish identity crisis helps you to cope with
other identity conflicts. One of the problems in
Ireland is that the Protestants have a very less clear
view of their identity than the Catholics and that
they are , in all-Ireland terms, a minority. We see
this in discussions and in our groups. The Catholics
were generally much clearer in their minds as to
what they wanted, compared to the Protestants.

One of the forms of the conflict is that people
are not equal partners. If people are equal or feel
themselves equal they can say what they feel even
if this is hard on the other partner. But if one
partner is weak, both may hide certain issues and
say 'Don't let's talk about them' or they don't even
see that certain issues are involved, they just don't
believe what the other partner is saying.

We have learned a lot on the issue of loyalty. How
far is it possible in Northern Ireland for the two
groups to take responsibility for each other's
history? Could the Catholics take on themselves,

take seriously, the Protestant history in Northern
Ireland – could the Protestants take on themselves
the Catholic history? This is an emotional question
which applies not just to Northern Ireland but which
can be asked of other countries and peoples.

In a certain sense everyone belongs to a cultural
minority and yet we have to live together in a
pluralistic society – the Irish question can teach us
all something. The loyalty issue is not typically
Irish, although it has its political roots in Northern
Ireland, but the loyalty issue is a basic human issue
so long as people from different cultures and loyalty-
systems have to live together.

In the Netherlands, for example, we have cultural
minorities like the South Moloccans and the people
from Surinam and we just don't know how things
will develop. If you look at history and at the great
civilisations, they emerged precisely at that point
where several influences were at work – the Middle
East, Europe, India, Central America, a kind of
cross-fertilisation which only takes place, among
other things, through conflict.

If the people of Northern Ireland succeeded in
transcending the old identities, in the sense of
taking them up with them and creating something
new this would have a tremendous influence in the
rest of Europe as a symbol of hope and as a reassur-
ance that a point of conflict can be overcome.

The conferences for the clergy were a particular
challenge because they were so much captives of the
prevailing situation that they could not move freely.
The conference with the Roman Catholic clergymen
was so far more difficult than that with the Protestants, which ran more smoothly and the clergy
had one or two follow-up meetings afterwards.

Perhaps the Protestants had more opportunities to escape from their backgrounds.

The real conflict arose in the Catholic conference because they felt betrayed by being confronted with Dutch Catholicism as they witnessed it in meetings with different groups or through visits to a number of Dutch parishes. The crucial point of that conference was the introduction of a lady from the Council on Church and Family of the Dutch Presbyterian Church and she gave a very short talk on family problems in the Netherlands. During the talk she used the term 'family planning'. That was dynamite.

The Irish clergy associated this with contraceptives, though these had not been mentioned. Perhaps the conflict that we had with this group was not totally a waste of time – many would have wanted to go home and to forget as quickly as possible what had happened but could they forget? We fear however, that it may have caused some people to cling even more to their values back home, to the Irish situation. Dutch society is so much more liberal and they had experienced a cultural shock. We underestimated the strength of that shock.

When you observe Irish clerics, the way they speak, the way they look at secular society, they are reminiscent of Dutch theologians of the Thirties, in that the church is not really in touch with developments of modern society. In private, Irish churchmen know that young people do not have the same attitude to the church as in the past, they know that things are changing, but no-one talks about this on the official level.

Also the attitude to Scripture and theology is very pious, very spiritual. The Churches in Ireland are living in a certain dichotomy – on one side there is the social, political and material life of the daily

world, and on the other side is the realm of the
spirit, of religion, of morals and these two elements
do not seem to have much relation to one another
in Ireland.

The emphasis is on the individual and the soul.
The fact that the social aspect of salvation is an
important part of scripture seems to be beyond most
churchmen in Ireland. The Catholics feel that it is
important to be a Catholic or at least a Christian,
whereas a more enlightened view might be that it
is important in every place to have some Christians
and that you have people who try to live the
Messianic life of a man who lives out of Scripture,
and that he should be in close contact with what is
happening in society.

The Irish church seems to be standing for
morality more than for the concept of liberation.
Moralists are always very afraid of life and they
translate that fear into morals, and that is what the
church in Ireland is doing. The churches there also
have a lot of temporal power, you can see it and you
can 'smell' it. They are an important social factor.

In one discussion group we talked about the rights
of Dutch youth, but one Irish participant said 'You
cannot talk about rights unless you talk first about
responsibility. Rights come after responsibility.'
That is moralism. You have to earn your rights, so
to speak, by taking up responsibilities. You have to
obey the law first, and then there is grace. That is
the theory of justification by works. This kind of
moralism is disastrous in Irish society and it comes
through again and again.

When Irish groups talk about peace there is also
a tendency to talk about peace as a personal attitude
– that peaceful people should not have an aggressive
part in their make-up. You should behave in a

peaceful way and that means behaving according to
certain moral standards, thus you translate peace
into a judgement of a person's qualities rather than
a relationship between two or more beings or
between two groups, and by moralising the whole
thing you prevent them from taking themselves as
they are, and the other person as he is. It's not
allowed.

This is part of the make-up of the authoritarian
person and the way people in Northern Ireland deal
with each other is rather authoritarian. The authoritarian person's convictions and values are like a
package that hovers above his head, but it doesn't
become part of him in such a way that he can live
with it. Someone in Holland said 'Faith is a parcel
that you deliver through to the next generation, but
you don't open it' and such a parcel becomes very
heavy.

The churches, as far as they are religious institutions, are captives of the social mores in which
they are functioning and, apart from having a
stabilising effect, they have a disastrous function.
The Irish or Gaelic identity is covered by the Catholic Church, the Protestant identity, as far as there
is one, is covered by the Protestant churches. So it
becomes very strange to be a Catholic and not to be
'Irish' or to be Protestant and not to favour union
with Britain.

In other words the church represents the nation,
or a certain group, or a certain class, but it does not
necessarily represent the church. So how can the
church be the church. . . ? By doing the impossible,
by again and again crossing the barriers. In Ireland
there is much contention and personal anguish over
marriages between Catholics and Protestants,
where in most cases the Protestant partner has to

promise to do all in his or her power to rear the children as Catholics.

This creates problems, and the barriers are there, and the churches are in some degree of conflict. What the true church should be doing is to encourage mixed marriages, to break down the barriers, to do the impossible. In schools people should not be taught first to become Catholics but to become human beings, or if they prefer, to become very good Protestants. People should be given help to choose, if they want to become Catholics or Protestants.

This new theology will come from the bottom, not from the top. Conflict can also mean change, and from despair there can be some hope – but not automatically. If despair means that you believe your own values and your own defences are not relevant any more and that you are faced with the fact that you may have to make a new start, then hope arises from a despairing situation. The fact that the old values don't apply and the existing structures don't work any more, this gives a chance to individual people and to small groups to take life in their own hands and become people who are going to make decisions.

In this way and in a conflict situation they have a great opportunity to influence history, perhaps much more than they think. If you want real renewal a lot of things have to happen – the old structure has to be broken down, the ground has to be cleared, a new foundation has to be laid and this will take time, but this is the way forward. That way there is hope from despair.

14

Search for Peace

The Reverend Dr Ray Davey is Founder of the
Corrymeela Community which was established to
promote reconciliation in Ireland and further afield.
Since 1964 the Community has organised meetings,
seminars, and family weeks for Roman Catholics and
Protestants at its Ballycastle headquarters in North
Antrim, while in Belfast there is an office to co-ordi-
nate work in the deprived urban areas. Corrymeela
has support groups in the rest of the United Kingdom,
the Irish Republic, Europe, North America and
Australia. Dr Davey is a Presbyterian minister, a
former prisoner of war in Italy and Germany, a
former chaplain at Queen's University, and a major
force in the practical work of reconciliation since
Corrymeela's inception.

CORRYMEELA began as a result of discussions
at the University, which is a great anvil for
ideas. I felt that the church needs to rediscover a
sense of community and I learned this from prison
camps during the war, and from communities like
Iona, Agape and Taizé. The churches had tended to
become very individualistic, with a piety concentrated on the individual's own spiritual welfare.

It was vitally important to rediscover the
togetherness of Christians. This togetherness was
very much a power in the early church, they

172 TRIED BY FIRE

supported and encouraged one another and were able to do things as a unit they would not have done as individuals. Fellowship is a terribly overworked word but that's what it is all about. It's like the golden grail, you are always looking for it, but it has never truly been found.

As a prisoner of war we had this togetherness and the experience obviously influenced me because when we started the student centre at Queen's I did not want it to be a one-man show, but rather the Christian presence at Queen's. That worked. I am moved to meet fellows on whom you had felt little impact had been made, but the impact was there. That's terribly basic to New Testament Christianity, and one of the things that the churches lost, particularly the Protestant churches, was the sense of togetherness. So one trend of Corrymeela has been the rediscovery of community.

The other strand was dealing with young people who were sophisticated and very critical. Most were in the church but they were looking very hard at the work of that church, which was doing little in the whole field of Christian unity. The idea of crossing the barriers between Roman Catholics and Protestants was very far in the background. But at Queen's University we gradually moved towards that.

In Ireland the events of the early part of the century, like the First Great World War and the creation of the Irish border, took an enormous amount out of the men and women of that generation. It was a very painful thing, and then it was reinforced by political division. As a young chap I remember almost no talk about the Irish question. We were orientated towards Europe; we were so much engrossed by what was happening there, the rise of Fascism, Hitler and Nazism, the Spanish Civil War. I remember doing a scholarship examination in September 1938 and debating whether there was any point in working because I was so certain there was going to be a war and I was wrong by only one year.

So Corrymeela was an attempt to meet the need for a Christian community, as well as an attempt to answer the urgent questions of these young people. Is the church to live to itself, or should the church be concerned about the world?

We visited other communities at Taize, Agape and Iona and we began to look for a place of our own in the Sixties. The important thing was to move from discussion and ideas to something concrete. After many discussions and meetings we decided to buy a building near Ballycastle on the North Antrim coast, and as soon as that decision was made we had to commit ourselves.

From the beginning the idea caught on with young people particularly and it did meet a need. The original idea was to bring people together in work camps. There was the physical task of cleaning the place up, putting the building in order. If we had had a marvellous building given to us we would not have been prepared for it. In a sense we found ourselves through the work that we had to do. There was the shared experience of working, and discussing and living together. And all the idealism of youth.

The first period was very much a local effort but gradually we drafted in people from other parts of Europe and America. I vividly remember the week that Czechoslovakia was taken over, we had six Czechs at Corrymeela and they were lying all day with their ears glued to transistor radios.

From the start we realised the importance of the Irish problem. The very first conference included the then Prime Minister of Northern Ireland, the audience was half Catholic, half Protestant but we set out to promote reconciliation at every level, in social terms, even in family terms between the generations.

When the violence broke out we were very aware of our limitations. In one sense our bluff was called because to a large extent we were not people who lived in the troubled areas. We were outsiders with a certain sense of powerlessness. But we began by bringing together the children from the flashpoint areas and then later on the adults. At least we felt that we were contributing something.

The violence caught up with us and our whole existence assumed a new meaning. Reconciliation was not only a much discussed concept but an issue in everyday life.

Looking back, we were certainly idealistic and visionary, though we never claimed we would solve the Irish problem or bring back peace. We saw our function rather to begin the process of reconciliation; pointing out the way; witness to what as a Christian Community we believed peace to be.

But there was one thing that was salutary for us as a Christian Community. Corrymeela from the start, by its very nature was about people and relationships. All sorts and conditions of people began to come to Ballycastle. So whether you like it or not you were brought face to face with the harsh brutal realities of the situation.

You not only talked to the young man who'd been 'done over' by the Paramilitaries and would never be a normal person again, but you lived beside him for several days. You stayed in the same building with a woman whose husband had been blown to pieces, or a young ten year old who was inconsolable because his father had been caught in cross-fire going to help a comrade. You spent several days talking to a family who had been intimidated and forced to flee from their home, and you listened in the course of the mealtime and other endless conversations to the accounts of all the different members of the family; you experienced the agony of the past, frustration of the present and the increasing apprehension about the future. You got to know the young lads who had to get away, or else. You felt the inner sickness that tormented them as they planned to go across the sea to a place where they had no friends.

Mothers opened their hearts to you as they talked about life in a ghetto situation − how they had to shut their children in lest they come to some harm. You heard the children scream with delight as they saw the sea in all its North Coast glory for the first time and heard them say when they came back from Ballycastle town after their first visit: 'Strange place that, no burnt out shops'. You agonised with the young teenagers about how they should or should not be 'involved' and how they could keep clear. Burned in your memory are those last days when the minibus was ready and they were going home. There were no dry eyes. Usually some of the boys ran away and tried to hide. You could never forget the seven year old child who was overheard to say, 'Goodbye sea, goodbye shore, goodbye heaven', as she prepared to go back to the multistorey in the inner urban areas. Then as well, all those who came from comfortable backgrounds who were deeply concerned and wanted to serve and give and care.

Corrymeela was all about people and so we did not have to sit and contrive projects and programmes −

they sprang out at us from all those real life
situations.

So began Family Weeks, Holidays for Pensioners,
and indeed the openness to families and individuals
who were 'at risk', and that can mean a multitude
of things.

So began the Summer Activities Programme
when four or five groups and projects ran concur-
rently with Work Camps, including Special Projects
for the handicapped. A great band of helpers came
from all over the world to cook, drive, organise arts
and crafts, recreation, music, worship. Step by step
the work in Belfast developed with it.

Soon we realised that we were only touching the
tip of the iceberg. We were only treating symptoms
– what about causes? So other people began to come
– community leaders, politicians, social and political
analysts etc. Thus we began the continuing process
of looking at the many social, political and religious
issues that lie behind the violence and unrest.

The outreach and the structure of the Community
developed. Various cells and groups have grown up,
and the staff at Ballycastle increased as the
programmes multiplied to cover a much wider range
of people. In Belfast a full-time Community Worker
and Youth Co-ordinator opened up many new areas
of work. There was also continual growth of interest
in and support for our work, not only in England,
but also on the Continent and indeed in America
and Australia.

One of the first key meetings involved young boys
who had never had a job. It made you realise what
unemployment did to them – it took away their
manhood, their sense of worth. But the really vital
meetings were the Family Weeks, when people from
both communities were brought together. The

strands of those weeks have stood the test of time.
We have become more sophisticated. The idea is to
bring together eight or ten families and we provide
preparation and skilled leadership, so they don't just
come to Corrymeela out of the blue. Very often they
are people who are not able to go on holiday otherwise. They live together, they share, they follow a
programme as well as have a holiday. One woman
with six children told me that she had not been
away from her home for one night in 18 years.

Of course there are basic choices to be made. Do
you go for the socially inadequate at the bottom of
the ladder — and we have done that — or do we
choose people who are potential leaders in their own
area? It's hard to separate them, but my inclination
has been to try to aim for the leaders. We have had
people to Corrymeela who would really have needed
a social worker with them. That can make life very
difficult, but we have learned from our experience
and we liaise more with the different welfare
authorities.

We have had families who would be sympathetic
to the paramilitary organisations. One week we had
two hard-line families who were committed to violence. At the start the Corrymeela workers wondered
if they could get through the week without real
trouble. But by the end of that week the families'
attitudes had completely changed. They had not
been given an opportunity to meet someone from
'the other side' before. The violence really does
polarise people. It's important to remember that it
takes a lot of courage for those people to move out
of their own areas even for a short time and the
tribal links are very, very strong.

So the families on this particular week discovered
that there was a common humanity which they

shared, they discovered that many of their problems
were the same. They learned from each other. And
they kept contact with each other afterwards. That
was a real victory. The best family weeks are those
which   produce   people   who   work   together
afterwards.

People say that Christians should naturally be
interested in reconciliation but when you are actually in a situation of conflict you have to think it
out. I have learned a great deal about the whole
theological basis of reconciliation and there is a
great deal still to be done in that area. From the
start Corrymeela was very pragmatic. We tried to
do good things and then thought a bit more deeply
about them afterwards.

The last few years had exposed the thinking of
the churches, how circumscribed it is. When you
think of the whole idea of Christian reconciliation,
and yet a vast group of Christian people is refusing
even to face up to the implications of crossing the
barriers between the Protestant and Roman Catholic traditions.

Community is building up trust and understanding and co-operation and love so that people
do things and celebrate their togetherness. All the
time we are learning in community and growing.
One can be idealistic and it does take a long time,
but I can see this beginning to grow, making this
Christian concept a reality not only as individuals
but together. To be a kind of a pressure group, to
stand up for certain things. We haven't gone public
on a lot of things because we felt that we could take
effective action more subtly.

A great deal can be done quietly. Once you go
public and attack people you put them under
pressure and they go on the defensive, but if you

move quietly and if you have enough credibility to make your case you will be heard.

Among the churches there has been a lack of prophetic leadership. A person can represent the views of his people and that's a kind of leadership, or he can lead them and try to get them to move out from a fixed position – that's what I mean by prophetic leadership. I'm not referring just to the heads of the four main churches but also to the clergy and laity. More could be done. A lot of people have become depressed and have opted out, and kept within their own tradition – which is very sad. The churches should be the instrument of reconciliation.

I have thought a great deal recently about Saint Paul's letter to the Ephesians. People should study that in depth, because it gives the theological background to God's whole plan and purpose which is to create a true 'comm'-unity, a true human family, and all of this has to be taken far more seriously. The church has to be the instrument of reconciliation that breaks down the barriers. What saddens me is that many times you can go into a church still and listen to a service that has very little reference to the current situation. It's hard to imagine the Old Testament prophets doing that – they always made it relevant to the situation of their day.

Our old friend 'pietism' is alive in Ireland in a big way. Everything is spiritualised, but this is a truncated Gospel. You have to be reconciled to Christ, to the church and to the world. This, of course, is not just an Irish thing, it exists world wide – the person who lives to himself 'my faith and my salvation' and on the other hand the faith that reaches out to the social and political order. It's vital for the church to weld these two strands together, because that is New Testament teaching – the one

gives you the motivation to do the other. And this
message must get through to the churches.

I hope that I've learned something about peace-
making. It is vitally important to strike up a
relationship with people and to help them where
they are. This is long, slow and painstaking work,
and it's not as simple as some people believe.

I've heard them say 'All you have to do is get
Catholics and Protestants together'. That is valu-
able but unless you have something more concrete
to occupy them the relationship can break down. It's
important to have issues which they can get their
teeth into.

Then there is the more intellectual side of peace-
making, and the whole area of 'conflict studies' and
'sensitivity groups'. This has its own contribution
to make. Then there are others who believe it's a
religious thing, and that there's a need to pray
harder, and to meet together as Christians. All
these things bring people together and make them
think more about reconciliation, but I believe that
you have to take a harder look – if only to see your
limitations.

You have to realise the things that you can do
effectively. Peacemaking has so many different
aspects. There is the political role and there has to
be a political compromise of some sort. One
important area is that of attitudes, how people
think. Their hopes, their fears, their anxieties, their
ambitions. It's those things that make up political
attitudes and I believe Corrymeela can operate here
to change attitudes and this is a long-term process,
but I don't see any other answer. There's a place for
peace studies, and a place for the whole Christian
dimension, but the area where you have a better
chance to change the structures is through atti-

tudes. If attitudes change, then structures will change.

So you bring peace largely from the bottom rather than from the top, although you must remember that we haven't actually got peace yet. We are still talking very much in theory, but I have seen attitudes change and what we are doing is absolutely valid; the only thing is that it should be extended and done much better.

The Irish question is not isolated because it's part of a far bigger problem. All over the world there is terrific unrest, there are all sorts of minority problems. The great idea of the Christian faith is that of creating a new society, a new comm-unity. This is the real question in the world, how can we learn to live together, how can we have unity in diversity.

Other countries have this embryonic problem. In England there is the whole question of the National Front and the different minorities, and many people in England are deeply worried about the alienation. If we can solve our problems in the North of Ireland we will have something very important to say to the wider world.

The trauma here may be the way that the Divine plan is working out, in that our problem is concentrated in a small area – but all the real issues are concentrated in a very violent form. Issues like identity, nationalism, and minorities. It is a tremendous challenge to the Christian conscience. The Christian has to rediscover the centrality of the message of reconciliation. So often the pietist is apt to think that man gets reconciled to God in Jesus Christ but the real crunch of the message is that if you believe that, you are part of the reconciliation between man and man. A lot of people stop at the first, and don't follow through.

The man outside Ireland as well as the man inside
Ireland has to think in those terms. We have to
realise that the technological age is now saying to
us that we are all one. All the big questions are
the international questions – the shortage of fuel,
ecology, hunger, the arms race. We are already in
a global village and we are dependent on each other.

The word Shalom sums it up, a balanced healthy
society. The thrust of the Christian message is that
of one true community, that's what it's all about
today. If the church has nothing to say about
reconciliation it has nothing to say at all. What is
the relevance of being concerned with your own
parish pump activities if the whole world is bleeding
to destruction?

Shalom has so many ramifications. The old
prophets were against a phoney peace, because it
was not tied to social justice. We have so much to
learn from that, we can't just paper over the cracks
– we have to strip it right down and look at our
society. Maybe one of the best ways to work for a
new society is to work for a just society. And this is
international, it is not just Northern Ireland.

I've been very moved by the help and interest
from English people, and touched by the concern for
us there. We appreciate the interest, and the money
they have given us, and the feeling they have
towards Ireland. Part of that is a feeling of guilt
among the more perceptive ones, and partly a belief
that the Irish are letting the Christian side down.
On the ecumenical front there is a feeling that this
Irish conflict is a disgrace to everyone, which it is.

This is a Western country where the most appalling things have been happening and they have
been happening allegedly between Catholics and
Protestants, although that's an over-simplification.

Coupled with the concern in England is a great degree of humiliation. English people will not tell us what they think we ought to be doing – they support us, pray for us and visit us, but they don't try to dictate to us. And this has been good. In Southampton they wanted me to comment about the situation locally, drawing from my experience, but I said 'I'll talk about Ireland and you can take from this what you feel is relevant for yourselves, but I would not dare to come into a place and comment on it directly'. A lot of people are taking the point. One fellow said to me 'What's happening in Ireland today could happen here tomorrow'.

One chap in Portsmouth – an Irishman – said he would rather walk down the Falls Road or the Shankill Road in Belfast than around his church at night, which is near the docks. There is a great deal of alienation in England, the muggings, the soccer violence, it can be quite shattering.

In trying to bring peace to Ireland in particular, people are wont to look at the big things. They say that it's up to the politicians, or the big community leaders. But in fact peace has to be a gradual thing, like a change in the climate. Something has to sweep right through slowly, and that depends on everyone in the churches and elsewhere beginnir g to build relationships.

We don't want people who say 'You're doing good work, here's a fiver for Corrymeela'. We want people who begin to work it out for themselves at their own level, building relationships with Catholics or Protestants, becoming friends. Not treating them as separate people or writing them off as some people do, without saying anything. That way it's building up from the grass roots.

It's also being aware of the social issues, knowing

about unemployment and realising that unemployment and violence go together, and asking what can be done about that, to look at how church buildings and resources are being used – all these kinds of things.

At the start maybe we all thought it was too easy. We have been forced to get down to the basic issues, that it's not just getting together and being nice to each other. We have realised that the search for lasting peace is much deeper.

Saint Paul has several very salutary things to say about this struggle. A most important point is his phrase 'We are not contending against flesh and blood, but against principalities and powers'. In other words, the problem is more complicated than it looks. It behoves us to avoid superficial analyses or easy answers. Paul is warning us to avoid 'short cuts'. We would do well to listen to Tehodor Haecker; 'Beware of the terrible light-hearted simplifiers. They create the most hopeless confusion in the long run'.

There's a lot to be learned from Ireland in a negative sense. What has happened here has been a judgement on pietistic religion. The church that won't face social or political issues can very easily be manipulated – and we haven't learned this in Northern Ireland yet. The church has to be prophetic, to stand out in social and political terms. It has to witness. Whether we succeed or fail is not in our hands to decide. What we have to do is stand for what we believe to be right. And people will know that by what we say and what we do. It's not so much to solve the question, but to be a sign of what we believe the Christian response to be at this particular time.

Yet when you look at the situation closely with a

terrific honesty and you strip it away to its basics, you have to ask the question 'Do we really deserve peace yet'? Are we still crying Peace Peace, where there is no peace? Are we prepared to pay the price for peace? Have we stripped away and removed the things that prevent peace from becoming a reality?

The price of peace is a removal of fear, the Protestant fear of the Catholic Church, the traditional Catholic fear of the Northern Ireland Protestant. Those fears have to be faced and this includes really courageous action at the ecumenical level. Are we going to be the instruments of exorcising fear, but without getting together, without being able to talk? If we remain polarised we will never be able to talk to each other. We are giants in the art of war but miserable pygmies in the arts of peace.

Despite the tragedies you can never really despair because there's always some light coming through. Recently I asked a well-known English politician if he despaired about this place and he said 'When you have an hour of prayer and Bible study each morning, how can you despair?' And I think he's right. God is in the situation and He is working His way through.

15

Epilogue

> True justice is the harvest reaped by peace-makers
> from seeds sown in a spirit of peace.
>
> (James 3:18. NEB).

IN ONE sense this book has no final chapter. It
has a recurring theme — "forever beginning".
There have been many profiles of hope amid the
despair of the dark story of Ireland. There have been
people down the years who have tried to point to a
peace for Ireland but it has been a hope thwarted
by the emotions of the past, the passions of the
present and the uncompromising reality of violence.

Today while hope ebbs and flows, dims and sometimes sparkles into the flickering of a possibility of
peace, the killing goes on. A young Irishman is shot
dead by terrorists as an alleged informer and his
body is left on the apron of an Irish bog. A gallant
old soldier and his son, both steeped in the British
tradition, are murdered in their stately home by
terrorists who display a chilling sophistication in
the modern weapons of war.

The sinister forces of history swirl ominously like
black clouds in a gathering storm. The battle-cries
of "No surrender" and "Not an inch" are the cacophany in the background of rifle-crack and bomb-
blast as more blood is spilled and another life ebbs

away. In the rich beauty of lakeland Fermanagh there is an ugliness and a poison as men live in fear of a terrorist bullet. On an Antrim hillside ranks of men stand in darkness to proclaim a fight to the death to defend what others deem indefensible. The reality and the symbolism are one.

Yet there is another form of reality, the freshening symbolism of hope. There is indeed another island, another Ireland, that lives and moves quietly beneath the noise of war. It is an island where human hands are reaching tentatively across human divides. The handshakes grow strong and they begin to build bridges. The bridges are small, but they are there.

Despite the gloom, the violence, and the evidence of inhumanity all around, the future cannot be without hope. Those who hold out the prospect of peace, who refuse to accept that war is the natural condition of the Irish or indeed mankind, can point to a better way which will require sacrifice on all sides. Whether their work can help to avert a catastrophe or whether the words and ways of peace are those which will build up a new society after a catastrophe is one of the major imponderables in the broad sweep of Irish history.

In the daily trauma of life in Ireland, the touchstones for the peace-makers remain faith, hope and charity. There is indeed faith, and there is charity, despite the warfare and the mistrust. And there is hope that refuses to disbelieve that peace, some day, will be a reality. But the words of William Butler Yeats are both a comfort and a warning for those soiled and wearied by the dust of history and the pollution of present times.

'And I shall have some peace there, for peace comes
    dropping slow,
Dropping from the veils of the morning to where the
    cricket sings;
There midnight's all a glimmer, and noon a purple
    glow,
And evening full of the linnet's wings.'

Peace will come, though dropping slow. A society
without hope is a society without a peaceful future.
The profiles of hope remain a witness to a far, far
better way forward for all.

THROUGH DAVID'S PSALMS

Derek Prince

Derek Prince, internationally known Bible teacher and scholar, draws on his understanding of the Hebrew language and culture, and a comprehensive knowledge of Scripture, to present 101 meditations from the Psalms.
Each of these practical and enriching meditations is based on a specific passage and concludes with a faith response. They can be used either for personal meditation or for family devotions. They are intended for all those who want their lives enriched or who seek comfort and encouragement from the Scriptures.

LOVING GOD

Charles Colson

Loving God is the very purpose of the believer's life, the vocation for which he is made. However loving God is not easy and most people have given little real thought to what the greatest commandment really means.
Many books have been written on the individual subjects of repentence, Bible study, prayer, outreach, evangelism, holiness and other elements of the Christian life. In **Loving God**, Charles Colson draws all these elements together to look at the entire process of growing up as a Christian.
Combining vivid illustrations with straightforward exposition he shows how to live out the Christian faith in our daily lives. **Loving God** provides a real challenge to deeper commitment and points the way towards greater maturity.

If you wish to receive *regular information* about *new books,* please send your name and address to:

London Bible Warehouse
PO Box 123
Basingstoke
Hants RG23 7NL

Name _____

Address _____

_____

_____

_____

I am especially interested in:
- [ ] Biographies
- [ ] Fiction
- [ ] Christian living
- [ ] Issue related books
- [ ] Academic books
- [ ] Bible study aids
- [ ] Children's books
- [ ] Music
- [ ] Other subjects

P.S. If you have ideas for new Christian Books or other products, please write to us too!